LIFE TOUCHES LIFE

More Praise for
Life Touches Life

In my own life, I have seen how the excruciating pain of the loss of a child can twist a woman's soul. I have also seen, in the pages of this book, how it can melt the walls of a Mother's heart, exposing the rarest kind of beauty and grace. *Life Touches Life* is an exquisitely beautiful story that carries the reader through the darkest of hours into the brilliant light of faith, hope and eternal love.

—Lone Jensen, Author, *Gifts of Grace*

Life Touches Life is a beautiful book. Told with gut-level honesty, it is a journey from love to loss and back into the light. It's simply a must-read memoir.

—Pat Carr, Author, *If We Must Die*

There is immense pain here, huge loss, and a searing loneliness. Yet the beauty of Lorraine Ash's account shows how hope, healing, and new possibility can be harvested from the terrain of sorrow. Eventually, the sore of grief becomes a well of presence.

—John O'Donohue, Author
Anam Cara: A Book of Celtic Wisdom

Lorraine Ash's book is important, insightful and moving. It will touch the heart of anyone who has ever had to cope with stillbirth, of course, but it will also deeply affect any reader who has suffered profound loss of any kind.

—Adam Pertman, Author
Adoption Nation: How the Adoption Revolution Is Transforming America

I highly recommend this superbly written, enlightening, and inspirational story to everyone, no matter what their age, gender, or life circumstance. It is a deeply touching story of the boundless depth, resilience, love. and wisdom of the human spirit.

—John E. Welshons, Author
Awakening from Grief: Finding the Road Back to Joy

LIFE TOUCHES LIFE

A MOTHER'S STORY OF STILLBIRTH AND HEALING

BY LORRAINE ASH

Foreword by
Christiane Northrup, M.D.

NewSage Press
Troutdale, Oregon

LIFE TOUCHES LIFE:
A Mother's Story of Stillbirth and Healing
Copyright ©2004 Lorraine Ash
ISBN 0-939165-50-3
EAN 978-0-939165-50-6

NewSage Press
PO Box 607
Troutdale, OR 97060-0607
503-695-2211

website: www.newsagepress.com
email: info@newsagepress.com

Cover and Book Design by Sherry Wachter
Printed in the United States on recycled paper.

Distributed in the United States and Canada by
Publishers Group West 800-788-3123

PUBLISHER'S CATALOGING INFORMATION

Ash, Lorraine.
Life touches life : a mother's story of stillbirth and healing / by Lorraine Ash ; foreword by Christiane Northrup.—1st ed.
    p. cm.
ISBN 0-939165-50-3
1. Ash, Lorraine. 2. Mothers—Biography. 3. Stillbirth—Psychological aspects. 4. Loss (Psychology) 5. Grief. I. Title.
RG631.A78 2004
155.9'37'0852—dc22

                                                2004002818

2 3 4 5 6 7 8 9 10

W. ASH

IN MEMORY OF

VICTORIA HELEN ASH
stillborn June 2, 1999

her aunt
MAGGIE ASH
stillborn October 9, 1956

her cousin
MEAGHAN STANWOOD
b. March 22, 1984 - d. March 26, 1984

her cousin
THEODORE FRANKS MULLICA
miscarried September 11, 1997

CONTENTS

FOREWORD

*T*his is the most hauntingly beautiful, honest, and inspiring story of loss, grief, and transformation that I have ever read. I couldn't put it down and read it in one sitting. Within these pages I found good and powerful medicine for anyone who is in the crucible of grief, experiencing their hopes and dreams burned away by forces they cannot control. This book will give you solace. It will give you hope. Ultimately, this book is a celebration of life with all its pain, poignancy, and mystery. Lorraine Ash's story is validating, uplifting, and bracing. It felt good to know that someone else understood what I had experienced even though my path and my circumstances were entirely different.

When I went into labor with my first daughter, I had not made any preparations for her arrival. I had not bought a single item of baby clothing or furniture—not even a diaper or a T-shirt. Having spent the prior four years as a resident physician in obstetrics and gynecology, I certainly was well-versed in the needs of newborns and their mothers. However, during my eight years of medical training, I had internalized a very effective mind-body split—I didn't think that personal needs applied to me.

Toward the end of my pregnancy, the labor and delivery nurses began to ask if I had the baby's room ready yet. I always answered, "No." They would ask, "Where is she going to sleep?" I replied, "I guess we can put her in a drawer lined with a blanket or something."

Looking back, I see clearly that my lack of preparation for Ann's birth was an intellectual defense against the potential pain of an unforeseen outcome—a stillbirth or newborn death. I had seen one too many women suffer the loss of a baby and then have to go home and endure the pain of entering an empty nursery. I was convinced, albeit unconsciously, that if I didn't allow myself to emotionally invest in having and loving my baby, I wouldn't feel so bad if the baby died during labor or shortly thereafter. Rife with objective knowledge, but short on the wisdom of my own heart, I honestly believed that if my baby were stillborn, I could just leave the hospital and not have to deal with any reminders of her at home.

Thinking back on how successfully I managed to maintain my illusion of control by hardening my heart to both myself and my daughter during our pregnancy together, I am moved to tears of both regret and compassion. I missed out on our first nine months together and that is sad. Yet that attitude is not surprising given my medical training and also our cultural legacy around stillbirth.

One of my most vivid memories from residency was when I helped one of the senior attending physicians at the stillbirth of full-term identical twin girls. Each had become entangled in the other's umbilical cord during labor, forming a knot that cut off their blood supplies. The babies were absolutely beautiful with their rosebud lips and perfect little fingers and toes. Every cell of my being knew that it was important for their mother to spend some time holding her babies and acknowledging their short life. Intuitively I knew this was a way to begin her grieving process. So while my professor was stitching up the mother, I wrapped each of the twins in receiving blankets.

As I began to take the babies over to their mother, my professor stopped me abruptly, saying, "She does not need to see those children. It will not help her. You will not be showing her those children. It will only make it worse." I was asked to leave the room while he had the nurses remove the babies. The doctor was the authority, and his word was unquestioned. He was certain he was right, that seeing her babies would be harmful to the mother. The doctor meant well, but I knew that his approach was wrong. Like me with my first pregnancy, this doctor was under the illusion that we can successfully use intellect to control the pain of unexpected loss and grief.

Few events in life are as shattering to our illusion of control as the death of a baby whose health is affirmed over and over again by the best technology available. Yet babies still die during pregnancy even when their mothers have done everything right and all the tests are normal. What is more maddening is that an exact cause of death often remains unknown. I have come to see that our over-reliance on technology in medicine is nothing more than an extension of our illusion of control. No matter how many tests we run, or how sophisticated our technology becomes, they can't save us from the process of life. And the process of life always involves loss, loss that must be felt as the first step toward healing it.

In *Life Touches Life*, Lorraine Ash writes eloquently about the need to release the intellectual death-grip on the illusion of control following her daughter's stillbirth. Letting a mother see her stillborn baby evokes a deep emotional response that can be difficult to witness, especially if it elicits one's own pain. It is difficult to feel one's terrible powerlessness over stillbirth. Control is lost as the grieving process begins in howling earnest.

The approach to loss that too many of us have inherited from our families and our culture is, "Better to simply shield one's eyes, keep a stiff upper lip, and put the whole thing behind you as soon as possible." This approach is especially invoked when it comes to a stillborn baby. Though tempting, it simply doesn't work. Feeling the pain of what we've lost is the only way to deep healing. I now know there is no way to avoid the painful process of grief after a significant loss. Feeling this pain is facilitated by walking into an empty nursery or holding one's stillborn child. Because the pain and sense of loss can't get any worse, facing it begins to help the healing.

Lorraine Ash invested herself—body, psyche, and soul—in her relationship with her unborn daughter Victoria from the very beginning. Her bonding process with Victoria was aided immeasurably by the very technology that, in the end, couldn't save her. By the time Victoria's day of birth arrived, she and her mother were good friends with the dream of a lifetime of joy and co-creation ahead of them. Lorraine writes, "It's funny what you can know just by feeling a soul."

But up until very recently, a parent's grief over a stillborn baby hasn't been acknowledged or validated by our society. Instead, it has been hidden away—its sufferers urged to get on with their lives long before they are ready. The grief associated with the loss of a child who has lived in the world is lightened when this loss is shared with understanding friends and family. But when it comes to stillbirth, few know what to do or say to offer support because they haven't had the chance to bond with the child themselves. What is more, there are no culturally approved containers for grieving the loss of someone who has never lived outside the womb and never been welcomed into her greater community through spiritual or family rituals.

In their ignorance, well-meaning friends often make the grieving process worse by implying that loss of a pregnancy isn't serious or devastating because "you can have another one." They also indulge in their own illusion of control by assuming that the outcome could have been prevented by *different* medical care or *something* the mother herself could have or should have done. Lorraine deals with the difficulties of this head-on without flinching. I applaud her.

Every loss that isn't grieved deeply stays with us. Time doesn't heal them. Instead, our griefs wait for us to feel and release them. We don't truly move beyond them until we really grieve. When we stop and grieve, then we begin to recover. Often, something miraculous begins to happen that imbues our lives with more meaning, feeling, and light than one can possibly imagine. I know this from my own experience of losing my sister and my father in the same year, and more recently, from losing my twenty-four-year marriage. Lorraine writes about this part of the recovery process so beautifully, I was moved to tears.

By allowing ourselves to experience the depths of our pain, releasing it little by little over time, we also find that we begin to experience a level of peace and joy we have never known before. Lorraine writes about this eloquently: "What my cousin Kathy told me is true. This awful heavy tragedy starts to feel, at times, like a rare joy, a gift. A light in my window on a winter night....I did not know that understanding is found in the feeling and that both come in a rush. I know now."

Recovering from a significant loss works other significant magic. It gives you x-ray vision for authenticity in another—letting you know instantly what is surface adornment and what is not. Grieving also makes you aware of the preciousness of time and of the life you have left. Lorraine tells how she learned these lessons from those who passed through her life as she grieved. In turn, we get to share in those lessons born from Lorraine's deep grief as we turn the pages of this book.

Thank you, Lorraine Ash, for allowing yourself to feel your loss so acutely and then for taking the time to distill it into such a moving piece of work. Thank you also, little Victoria Ash. Your brief physical life and untimely exit are a stunning example of how powerful a teacher one tiny being can be for thousands of others who never met you.

—CHRISTIANE NORTHRUP, M.D.
Author, *The Wisdom of Menopause*

LIFE TOUCHES LIFE

CHAPTER ONE

❧

The Joy of Anticipation

*I*t was a sparrow that caught my attention. I watched him as he hovered at the window, studying me. As I looked up and returned his gaze, I rubbed my belly, bursting with child at nine months. *Once again the birds are surrounding me,* I thought, *my emissaries from above.* Then I turned back to the business at hand—adjusting the baby crib sheets. These were the final days of waiting for my precious baby Victoria.

As I busied myself tending to the final details of preparing the nursery, the sparrow's visit stayed with me, alighting on memories of other birds and their visitations throughout my life. Once, in the purest moment of my girlhood, I stepped into a dove garden in Kyoto, an open redwood structure that swooped like a graceful Japanese character. Cooing doves perched everywhere on green branches—white delicate pillows who looked long at each other and at me. I did not understand the experience, yet I was soothed in the garden's mystery.

It seems I have always been soothed by the presence of birds. My grandfather raced homing pigeons. Together we would sit on the fire escape of his apartment as he ate his dinner on fine china set on a white linen cloth spread on a stool. While he ate we watched the horizon for the pigeons to come home. When they appeared as specks in the distance, he smiled with a deep satisfaction at their return, and rushed downstairs to greet and feed them.

My father's Bible, the one he held at church, showed a blessed bird. He taught me that the Holy Spirit—a Christian aspect of God—sanctified and enlightened us with rays of love from his divine wings. Years later, I learned the ancients also considered birds divine messengers. They believed birds could carry souls between this world and the next.

As a young woman with her feet planted firmly on the ground I stopped musing on birds. I no longer looked up. But on this particular morning, I noticed. I was forty years old, ready to birth my first baby. June 1, 1999 was to be the greatest day of my life, the day Victoria Helen would enter the world. This was the day she and I, friends from long conversations and walks, souls already fused, were to meet in the flesh.

It was one week past my due date and intermittent labor pains had started in earnest the night before. Tuesday morning, my husband Bill and I went to the obstetrician's office. The plan, the doctor had said, was for me to go into the hospital that day and for him to induce labor. We had tried to induce labor two weeks earlier simply because the doctor thought it was good practice to do so. A hormonal gel had failed to soften my cervix then and we had not even gotten as far as using Pitocin, the synthetic hormone that triggers contractions and sets birth in motion. "Why force things?" we all had agreed two weeks earlier. "Let nature take its course."

The first time I was in the hospital I had noted that the doctor always used the word "plan" when he discussed the impending birth. In retrospect, it was a good word. People plan. Nature dictates. Victoria and I had done so well together for nine months. There were a few times she put too much pressure on my kidney in the seventh month, and I would double over in sharp pain, but we had gotten through that scare. Monitors always showed her heartbeat to be vigorous.

Victoria was our little Sweetlet, as her father called her. Throughout the pregnancy Bill would come home at night from his computer job or one of his jazz trumpeting gigs, take off his trademark Crocodile Dundee hat, put his face to my abdomen and say, "Hi, Sweetlet, it's me, Dad. I'm the fun one. I'm the one who's always right." Then, later, before bed, he would say, "We can't wait to meet you, Sweetlet. Come out soon, okay?"

In the two weeks between scheduled inductions we were happy, anxious, awestruck, and tender. Bill sketched my swelled belly in charcoal, called it Victoria's first portrait and placed it on the changing table. After her birth we planned on hanging the drawing on the nursery wall. Bill had taken to doing things like that.

Downstairs in the living room he commandeered the white message board and drew a family tree for Victoria so she would know her first name came from her mother's side of the family and dated back to her great-great grandmother, Vittoria, who spelled it the Italian way. Victoria was the middle name of the baby's mother and her grandmother. Baby Victoria's grandfather was Victor Philip and her uncle Theodore Victor.

The baby's middle name, Helen, had a similar significance on the Ash family tree. It was the middle name of Victoria's paternal grandmother, her aunt's name, and the name of both her great-great grandmothers. Victoria Helen was a name steeped in tradition. "It's a name she'll appreciate," Bill would say, smiling.

One morning before Bill left the house, we hugged and kissed as we always do. When he got to the door, he turned and glanced my way. "We've been so happy, just the two of us," he said. "It'll be different with Victoria, even more wonderful with our Sweetlet." To us, our first baby felt destined to be in the world. When finally we felt ready for parenthood, we conceived on our first try. I was thirty-nine and Bill forty. The first clue we had succeeded revealed itself on a mountaintop in Acadia National Park in Maine where we had been hiking with my friend, Mark, and his girlfriend in September 1998. The last day of our hike I stopped to catch my breath more than usual. On the long drive home from that vacation, waves of nausea kept washing over me. "God, what's the deal with this?" I said to Bill. "Maybe it was something we ate at lunch."

"Maybe you're pregnant," he said, and we looked at each other and grinned.

"Wishful thinking," I replied. "It would never happen so fast." When I walked in the door of our house, I went straight for the pregnancy kit. The result was positive.

Amniocentesis a couple of months later revealed we were having a girl. For some reason, we had been convinced we would have a boy and Bill had been revved up about toy cars and steam train rides on autumn afternoons. Now Bill had to adjust to having a girl—not that his adjustment took very long. Within a week he was aglow with the idea of holding a daughter, and a kind of gentleness overtook him whenever he spoke of her.

I wondered if I looked different when speaking of her. I guess I must have. I spoke to Victoria, and about her, all the time. Friends felt as if they knew her. One afternoon my friend Brian visited me at the newspaper where I worked and mused about what she might become. "Victoria Helen," he said. "Maybe a romance writer. No, the name's too upper-class-sounding. An English professor, yes, that's it."

In Chicago, Mark, who already felt like an uncle, was talking up a storm about Baby Victoria to those who worked for him. "They all think I'm crazy," he said. "They nod, of course, but they're looking at me like, 'Who cares?' Well, I do. I care."

Everyone we knew was gearing up for Victoria. My college friend, Lisa, began buying baby dresses fit for a princess. "I showed one to my mother," she told me one day, laughing. "My mother said, 'Great, Victoria can wear it when she goes to Buckingham Palace.'" My husband's cousin, Christine, who had planned the baby shower, was as excited as a second mother. Karen, my writing buddy, referred to my baby as "Little Miss Victoria."

Victoria's grandmother, or Nonna in Italian, bought her an apricot-colored dress with a smiling white bunny grasping a carrot on the front as well as a green stretch suit with snaps. Under each snap was a little white bow with a pink flower in its center. Nonna relished the promise of long walks in Saddle Brook Park with her new granddaughter. Nonna and Nonno had purchased Victoria's nursery furniture, completing the baby's room. The changing table and crib were of a blonde wood and the crib was draped in beige bunting with hand painted, pastel-colored letters of the alphabet. A mobile of small, fluffy brown bears hung over the crib. I imagined Victoria sleeping in her crib, squirming as she awoke, her little eyelashes fluttering, her eyes focusing on the dancing bears. My father wanted to buy a variety of mobiles so she would have different pretty things to see. Already he declared he would call her "Queen Victoria."

My inner sense of Victoria was also one of excitement, anticipation, and a knowing that her soul was serene, lovely. I imagined that she would become a woman with a quiet, knowing smile, the kind of woman who would look deeply into a friend's eyes and really listen. Victoria would have an easy manner. She would slink onto a couch in jeans with as much grace as when she wore a fleece robe or a satin evening gown. Imagining the person that Victoria would become, I thought, *It's funny what you can know just by feeling a soul.*

That morning in the nursery when I saw the sparrow fluttering at the window I intuitively knew, *There's a message for me.* Exactly what it was, I did not know.

❀

CHAPTER TWO

A Heartbeat Away

*T*uesday morning my labor pains had started. They were intermittent but increasing in intensity. We stopped at the doctor's office, planning to head for the hospital to check in for the birth. While talking with the doctor, I mentioned, "You know, I haven't felt her move in the last day—just in the last day. I felt her move Sunday night."

He paused, looked at me for a few moments, then said, "Lie down. That's the last thing an obstetrician wants to hear. Don't tell me that."

I reclined on the examination table, still mostly relaxed, ready for my husband to drive me across the street to the hospital. So many friends had babies over the years and they all said it was normal for the baby to be still sometimes in the final stretches of pregnancy. *After all, the baby is so large and the elbow room she has so small, I reassured myself.* The doctor held his Doppler to my belly. Then he lifted the Doppler, re-gripped it, and listened again. And again. Then again. His jaw tightened.

"I'm not getting a heartbeat."

"What does that mean?" I asked.

The doctor responded, "Let me try again."

I looked at my husband. We said nothing. After another attempt, the doctor said, "Let's send you over to the hospital. Maybe it's just the way the baby's positioned. Maybe with the ultrasound equipment, they'll pick it up." Trying to sound reassuring, he added, "Let's not panic yet."

We did not panic. Bill and I walked out of the office in silence. We got in the car in silence. Bill started the car. I looked at him and his gaze met mine. "We don't know yet," I said, trying to sound buoyant. "We don't know anything yet."

"That's right," Bill said. "We don't know." We drove across the street, parked the car in the garage, and collected our hospital gear, which we had gleefully packed days before.

Neither of us spoke as we walked into the hospital. A polite quiet attendant brought a wheelchair, then wheeled me to the maternity ward as Bill walked alongside. Everyone appeared like one great mass of life moving around me in different directions. No single sound, just a collective, muddled noise as if the world were underwater. My eyes could not distinguish any face except Bill's. I looked up at him a million times and some of those times he would nod or pat my hand.

My mouth could not articulate one word. My whole being focused on a single, silent thought: *Where is my Victoria and what has happened to her?* Once in my room,

I put on the hospital gown. The floor was cold, the cement walls a cool encasement.

"The doctor couldn't find the heartbeat," I said to the nurse as I climbed into the bed. "Maybe you can." A young resident walked in. Her stethoscope slid over my stomach as the four of us looked at the monitor. On every ultrasound we had seen up to that point there had been movement, but now only stillness. The resident looked and looked.

"We have even bigger, better machines in Maternal Fetal Medicine," she said. "We'll try listening for it there." My doctor arrived and agreed we should use the more advanced equipment.

By now the coldness had seeped into me. Bill and I still said nothing. *Our baby, our beautiful little baby, could not have slipped away,* I told myself. *It is not possible. How could it be? Why would it be?* Victoria and I had passed every appropriate test known to the medical profession. Her heartbeat was strong just days earlier. Physically, I had felt fine the whole nine months. I had never stopped feeling fine. I had lived pristinely during the pregnancy. Victoria had the perfect environment to grow in and my genetic counselor had even taken the time to remark on that. I never smoked, drank, or took illegal drugs during my lifetime. What was happening?

The nurse wheeled me to Maternal Fetal Medicine as my husband once again walked quietly at my side. In silence, I lay down on the bed and looked around at the walls decorated with hundreds of photographs of babies and mothers. *Were they all born here? How could all these hundreds, thousands, of babies have been born here and how could mine not be born?*

Again they searched for a heartbeat. The high-tech monitor was silent—there was no heartbeat. No one would say the words, so I did. "So, you mean, my daughter is dead?"

"Yes," the nurse answered. She stared at me a moment, then looked away. "I'm going to leave you alone for a little while. I'll be back shortly." She handed my husband a form on a clipboard and asked him to fill it out. He took it from her, grabbed a pen from his shirt pocket, put the board on a shelf against the wall and started writing. It was still morning, only two hours since we had arrived at the doctor's office. *Could the whole world change that quickly?*

"I'm stunned," I said. "I am utterly stunned. I'm in shock." Then I heard a wail as my husband released the most primal, anguished sound I have ever heard. He dropped the pen, laid his head in my lap, and sobbed. He cried as if he could not stop. "I know, sweetie," I said, rubbing his back. "We came to love her so much. She was our little Sweetlet." Pictures of other people's sweetlets surrounded us as we held one another. I dared not cry—not with the reality of still having to deliver her corpse. *I will get through the physical part first*, I demanded of myself, *and I will dam up the tears until that ordeal is over.*

I was wheeled back to my room on the maternity ward, but it felt different. To me, this was the dying ward now and I was in the dying room. All hope had drained from it. My doctor decided to commence Victoria's delivery immediately so as not to prolong the agony for a minute longer than necessary. Within half an hour the doctor gave me an epidural in my spine, for which I felt grateful. I welcomed any lessening of the pain.

The first call Bill made was to his mother. I heard him say, "We lost the baby." The words reached me as if through a mist. *What is he talking about? How could I lose Victoria?* I thought. He dialed again and this time my father and brother were on the line. I pictured each at his own desk in their law office. They must have been smiling, expecting a burst of good news. I blurted it out. "Victoria died. They can't find her heartbeat."

The silence on the other end of the receiver was palpable. I heard my brother sniffle. He said, "What?"

"They can't find her heartbeat," I repeated.

My father spoke. "I don't know what to say. I just don't know what to say, Lorraine."

"I'll tell Mom," I said. Bill dialed and I heard the phone ring in my childhood home. My mother's cheerful voice answered. "Mom," I said, "Victoria has died. We lost her heartbeat." Again, that silence.

When my mother spoke she choked up. "Oh, my God," she said. "How could this happen to my daughter? To my own daughter? It didn't happen to me."

As the hours stretched into mid-afternoon Bill called family and friends. Most of the time he put the phone to my ear so I could speak to them, too. My body was punctured by so many needles, connected to so many monitors, that I was glad for the soft humanity of voice-to-voice contact. I needed it. Everything seemed so sharp.

Two hours later, the Pitocin continued to drip, but it was not working. My uterus seemed oblivious to it. So was I. I looked at the clock. It had no meaning. Then my cousin Kathy called. Her voice was soft but deep with years of grief and wisdom. Her little girl, Meaghan, had died fifteen years earlier when only a few days old.

"It feels like shit, doesn't it?" Kathy said. "It's outrageous. You have every right to be angry." I liked that but my upper lip was still stiff. I listened to her like I had listened to no one ever before. "Now Meaghan has a cousin in heaven," she said. "She's been up there a long time by herself and now she has somebody to play with."

That did it. I cried openly as Kathy went on: "When I left the hospital back then, I thought I had tried to make a baby and failed. Five years later, I'd tell you I had tried to make a baby and instead I made an angel. It's not a terrible thing to have your own angel, Lorraine. I know that sounds weird to you now, but you'll come to know it's true."

A wave of calm followed my phone call with Kathy, and time ticked on. At a little past midnight on June 2, the doctor decided to do a C-section. The operating room was cold as I lay under the scrutiny of a huge light. In my drugged, confused state, the light loomed like a large metal flower. *That's a medical flower,* I thought. The anesthesiologist told me to spread my arms on extensions that protruded from either side of the operating table. This was my crucifixion.

The eyes of the masked anesthesiologist searched my face as he asked repeatedly, "Are you all right?"

I said, "Yes," and I thought, *No.* I looked to the left and saw my husband's eyes, my only source of comfort. There had been times in my life when I knew I was close to falling into hell, but on that day I knew I had arrived. Silence entombed me. Only the soft sounds of voices padded that awful silence.

While the surgeon lifted Victoria from me, I reassured my husband. "This Friday we'll be sitting on the porch of our house and everything will be normal again. It will be hot outside and I'll make lemonade the old-fashioned way—the way we both like it."

He said, "Yes, of course."

I wanted normal. I wanted the baby back in my stomach. I wanted to try again.

I did not see Victoria then or in the recovery room. My semi-conscious haze precluded that. There was movement along with more lights on the ceiling that illuminated nothing, only blinded me. Nurses quietly walked around my bed, checking on drips and monitors. I had never felt so hot. My mouth was dry and I could only focus for a few moments at a time before closing my eyes.

Once I saw my husband, still in scrubs, follow a nurse out of the room. I remembered that earlier in the day he had said he wanted to hold Victoria while she was still warm from the womb and the nurse, I figured, was leading him to our daughter's body so he could do just that. He was talking as he left but his voice was a soft murmur of sound that faded into nothingness.

When he was gone, a nurse named Susan asked me how I was doing. "Your little girl," she said, "my goodness, she is beautiful. Such a pretty face. Pretty hands."

"I knew it," I said. "I noticed that on the ultrasound." Susan smiled. I smiled, too, but from a faraway place—a place of shock, pain, and heat from the life-threatening childbirth fever I had read about in history books. Here I was in 1999 in a modern hospital seriously ill with this same fever. Twenty-four hours earlier I was in the throes of joy and anticipation. At 1:30 a.m. in a hospital that had MRI machines and ultrasounds so sophisticated they had allowed me to look into the chambers of my unborn daughter's heart, I was now fighting for my life. *Is it possible for the tables to turn this fast?* I asked myself, my head reeling with fever.

My mind wandered between a distant world where Victoria somehow had gone, and the hospital where I lay, burning and weak. Another time when I opened my eyes my doctor was standing on one side of the bed and Bill on the other. They were talking about an infection and how I had it now. My temperature had soared to 103 degrees during surgery, and I was on an IV with three families of antibiotics in an attempt to kill the infection. I also had a morphine drip, which I could increase as needed with the push of a button.

My mind tried to grasp that the mystery of Victoria's death had been solved, but I could not absorb the information. In the depths of my being I could not comprehend how death could come so stealthily, and why I still felt its grip around my own body.

The doctor drew a likely scenario for Bill that I would comprehend much later: Group B Streptococcus bacteria, which occurs naturally, had seeped from the vagina through what probably was a microscopic tear in the uterus and infected it. The baby's head had then sealed in the infection. There had been no breaking of the waters. There had been no sign of trouble because the infection had been sealed in the uterus.

We would learn even later from the autopsy that this infection had caused Victoria to prematurely release meconium, the baby's first bowel movement that usually occurs soon after birth. The meconium contaminated the amniotic fluid, Victoria ingested it, and she slipped away in silence.

CHAPTER THREE

✤

Holding Victoria

The night of the C-section all explanations were beyond me. I was happy only to see a little smile on Bill's face when I asked him if he had held Victoria. He nodded yes, knowing I could comprehend no more than that. A kind nurse named Melissa pushed my bed into the maternity ward. She and an orderly were discussing how to get me from my recovery bed to the maternity bed, and I offered to help. "I'll just get up and sit on that bed," I offered. They looked at me blankly. "No, dear," the nurse said. "You're not able to do that right now. We'll figure it out."

After they lifted me from one bed to the other, the nurse stayed in the room. She looked at me kindly. "Mrs. Ash," she said, "you are a strong woman." That is when I found out that strong women have no idea who they are.

It was a full day before I held Victoria. Thursday was to be the day of her baptism, which a hospital bereavement counselor recommended because it would be difficult after that to keep her body from decomposing. I was ready. I had looked at the picture of Victoria the counselor had given Bill so I knew what she looked like. Bill and I decided we would meet with Victoria separately, and then together. After that we would have the baptism with the two of us and my parents present. My mother-in-law, whose second baby had been stillborn, did not want to participate. Already it was clear that grieving had many ways to express itself, and I began to understand that everybody's way was right.

I met with Victoria first. Without a word the counselor placed her heavy little body in my arms and then walked out, leaving the two of us alone. I was thrilled to see her and felt such satisfaction at holding her. "Oh, look at my brave little girl," I said. "Aren't you pretty? Oh, I knew you'd be pretty, Victoria. You were so brave to fight that infection, my *piccolina* (little one). How could you have won? Mommy is forty and healthy and she still can't fight this. How could you have won? I'm sure you put up a good fight, though, didn't you?"

I brushed my finger against Victoria's cold, soft skin and her crimson lips, the only sign that she was dead. Then I brought her up to my face and smelled her. The staff had powdered her up so much, she smelled alive. Victoria's face was pink and vibrant, even hearty. *If only she would open her eyes.* The nurses had dressed her in a diaper and white shirt. On her head was a white knit cap with a pink, blue, and white pompom on top.

Cradling her close to me, I whispered, "You remember, Victoria, you remember if you can, that Mommy loves you very much. We've been talking to each other for a long time now, haven't we, sweetie? Why don't we just keep doing that?"

Then I sat and rocked her, as mothers do. After a time, I had the most perfect moment of my life: I simply kissed her cheek. As I did, my heart filled. All these nine months, all the planning, all the anxiety, and all the joy and the love had led to a perfect kiss. I knew she was in the room watching. Victoria was there.

Then Bill joined me, and held Victoria. As he held his daughter he began to talk to her with the tender voice of a new father. "Hi, Sweetlet," he said. "It's me, Dad." But he could not finish the rest of the fun little speech he had recited to her so many times when she was in utero. He could not bring himself to say that he was the fun one, the one who was always right.

After we had about fifteen minutes alone with Victoria, my parents arrived and we all sat with her. My father said he could not get the story of Lazarus out of his head. "Why can't she just rise up?" he asked. "That'd be challenging God and you can't do that, but why can't she just rise up?" I did not know, but it was a fine question. A nun and the bereavement counselor came in next. As my mother held Victoria, the nun put a white and red bib on my daughter. "I baptize you," it said. The nun recited prayers over Victoria and made the sign of the cross with holy water over her forehead, welcoming her into the Christian community. I don't know what the nun said. Rote prayers from a very old ritual, but I was proud of

Victoria then and told her inwardly, *You will always be a part of this family who loves you so much.* Mostly, I used those few minutes to look at her. I did not know if I would see her again, ever again, and I wanted to memorize everything about Victoria.

What hands, I thought, *what exquisite hands.* Victoria held them over her heart, one below the other, with such grace. I saw her resemblance to me and I thought, *No one in the world will ever look like she looks.* I wondered if my mother saw the resemblance. I did not ask, though, because I was afraid my mother would say yes and that would have been unbearable. I watched as my mother handed my baby back to the bereavement counselor, as the counselor nestled Victoria gently amid the blankets in the wheeled hospital cart, as the cart moved out of the room. I knew I never would see her again. There was nothing the staff could do to stop the rapid decomposition of her body after that. The process, they said, already had begun, which is why I did not unwrap my baby from her clothes. I did not want to see that. I wanted to remember her as whole.

After Victoria was taken away, it was as if the light had left the room. I cried. My father sat on the bed next to my chair and thanked the nun for performing the baptism. The nun looked at me and shook her head. She said something about never being the same again.

"My daughter is a writer," my father told her. "She's written for years. She's written some plays." The nun looked at him as if to ask what that had to do with anything. He went on. "If you read them, you'd know the kind of spirit she has. She has some spirit, Sister. My daughter is going to be all right." The words had power for me. Everything my father had ever said to me was true.

Through all this time I held the big metaphysical questions at bay although they were growing inside my heart. *Why? Tell me why.* It was impossible to grieve my child and contemplate the mysteries of the universe. *One thing at a time*, I told myself. *Once the trauma itself has passed I can carry on with the spiritual exploration.* Yet, I knew even then, Victoria's death would be a crater in the landscape of my life.

CHAPTER FOUR

❁

In the Grip of the Fever

*M*y infection persisted. I was in the hospital for much longer than the time allotted for a C-section. Three days passed, then six, then nine, as the mystery of how to break my fever went on and on. Those days were a surreal haze of injections, cramps, and sweat. My intestines stopped functioning and for awhile I could not distinguish between a uterine contraction and a gas pain, so tangled were my agonies. My temperature vacillated from 98 to 103 degrees. That fever clung and I wondered, after a time, *Am I clinging to this fever because it is the only thing I have left that my daughter and I physically shared?*

One day when my mother visited I saw a look of alarm pass over her face as she regarded me. I was dressed in a white hospital gown with light blue flowers. In as long as it took for her to kiss me and sit down, the flowers on my gown turned dark blue from my fevered sweat. A nurse helped me out of the gown and gave me a new one, which darkened in another ten minutes.

My only solace was waking at night and seeing Bill asleep in the corner of the room, stretched out over two chairs pushed together and a blanket over him. On the screen of the overhead TV glowed silent reruns of "Star Trek," one of life's pleasures for us. I could not look at it for more than ten minutes without falling asleep. My concentration would not allow it. The copy of *The Art of Happiness* I had brought to the hospital similarly beckoned from my bedside table. The Dalai Lama's face smiled from the cover. I had gotten as far as putting a bookmark in the chapter on suffering.

The doctor had told my husband and me that we had every right to be angry. In those long nights, as my husband slept and the monitors all around me slowly clicked and hissed, I questioned, *Angry at what? At whom? At God?* God was the first option, of course, but one I could not accept. I had to choose a target, though, and, after the first few days, I chose the fever. It was what had killed Victoria. It was what was threatening to kill me. I hated this fever, and, internally, silently, I gathered enough strength to be angry at it.

Once my intestines started working again after several days, I could walk around the maternity ward for the first time. I had asked to stay in the maternity ward even though the staff suggested I should be somewhere else. There was one thing of which I was certain: I wanted to be around mothers and babies. I knew from the outset that happy mothers and their newborn darlings would be the most difficult sight for me to endure and I knew that if I could learn to face them at the outset I could face anyone and anything. I knew the mothers and babies were the ultimate test, the doorway I had to walk through on the road to wellness. I did not want to avoid that passage. I did not want to be coddled and protected in my horribly weak state only to feel a little better, a little better yet—and then face that doorway and collapse into ultimate agony again.

Well acquainted with my style of facing down problems after ten years of marriage, Bill did not question my decision to walk the maternity ward. He helped me walk it. I hobbled, bent over, as I leaned on his arm and clutched my IV pole. "IV-driving" Bill called it. He made me laugh, but what I beheld on the maternity ward did not.

During that first walk a nurse stopped me when I was about to turn a corner and pass the nursery. "Mrs. Ash," she said. "Don't go there. Not there, where the babies are. It will not be good." I responded, "So I'll pass the nursery. Babies are supposed to be in the nursery, not in the morgue. The mothers are supposed to be here, too. I'm a mother."

Very slowly I walked around and around the nursery, passing the rooms of the other mothers along the way. My room was far down at the entrance of the ward, removed. The babies did not cause me pain, but walking past the rooms did. I heard new mothers in those rooms:

"Not another colicky baby! I can't take it." *I will,* I thought.

"More balloons? It's too crowded in here." *At least you have something to celebrate*, I thought.

"I said this the last time. I don't like these soaps. I'm supposed to take a shower with these soaps?" I wondered, *Is this how we sound to God when we pray? Do we sound like people offering up a whining litany of self-absorbed complaints?*

As my walk wound down I had to pass the room next to mine. In it sat a very young mother, her face fixed like stone, a single small plant forlornly atop her tray table. Her baby was in her arms but she did not look at the child, did not cuddle, did not kiss. Clearly she was not happy. I never talked to her, I never heard her story, and I never saw anyone visit. I thought of the array of sympathy flowers that lined my room, of the company I had. *What kind of fate is it*, I thought, *that delivers an unwanted child and dispatches a wanted one?*

I walked more as the days went on, during the times the fever went down. The nurses on the ward became my personal cheering section. As Bill and I slowly shuffled through the halls they seemed to come out of the wood-work to applaud, sometimes literally. "Mrs. Ash, you be doin' it!" they said. "Way to go, Mrs. Ash!" A day nurse, Terry, told me stories about her sons when she changed my IV. The stories did not bother me, I suppose because her children were older—pre-teens. They were not babies. When Terry heard the soft James Taylor music I had playing in my room, she told me she was a fan, too. JT's music always had a way of seeping into my soul and working magic there. It was no different in the hospital when he sang:

In my mind I'm gone to Carolina
Can't you see the sunshine
Can't you just feel the moonshine
And ain't it just like a friend of mine
   to hit me from behind
And I'm gone to Carolina in my mind

As a kid I had been to Carolina once and I pictured what it had been like when I got up alone one night in the cool darkness and stood on the balcony watching the moonlight silhouette the docked boats as they rocked gently on the water. I went there in my mind and sleep took me. When I awoke in the evening another nurse, Leonie, spoke to me in her lilting Jamaican voice, encouraging me gently.

Bill and I made some decisions during those days, including the one to have our baby cremated. Victoria's body was moved from the hospital morgue and taken to a funeral parlor of our choosing. We would worry about the arrangements later but for now we concentrated on whether I would live.

A week and a half after the delivery my fever continued to quell and rise. My doctor came to my room to remove the staples from the C-section. He tried to calm me as he sat on the bed and raised my gown. "Don't worry," he said. "This won't hurt a bit." He smiled with his crystal blue eyes and patted my hand.

He suggested that maybe being home would help me feel better, and maybe the fever would subside there. The following morning I was ready to go.

CHAPTER FIVE

❀

Going Home

An attendant wheeled me to the front lobby where I waited for my husband to bring the car to the front door. I sensed movement behind me and turned to see another mother being wheeled toward me. She and I sat, together, waiting for our rides. She held a baby girl, Katlyn Nicole, and her chair was loaded with flowers and congratulatory balloons streaming behind her. She was beaming when she spoke to me. "Say, weren't you in Maternity?" I answered that I was. "Where's the baby?" she asked.

"The baby's dead," I said.

"Oh, no," she said. "I'm so sorry." Then, she added, brightly, "Don't worry. It happens. You'll have another one."

Then she was gone.

Every bump in the road on the ride home shot a pain up through my stomach. The beaming mother's remark played over in my mind. *It happens? Sure, but not to everyone.* When I got home, the fever had not yet passed.

— 31 —

My breasts, large and heavy, hurt; a pink, shiny fungal rash, the result of taking so many antibiotics, had blossomed under them.

There were so many flowers and plants in my house that it felt eerie, like a wake. The dining room was ringed in flower arrangements, expressions of sorrow, condolences—a loss of what to say. It looked like the viewing room of a funeral parlor. I slowly circled the dining table for a few minutes, then rushed out the front door as fast as my swollen ankles would take me. Somewhere between my house and the next, I heard two words: "I'm sorry." No one was around. I looked up and saw Samantha, my neighbor's cockatoo, peering at me from inside a bay window. "I'm sorry," she repeated in her familiar screechy voice, her yellow-crested head bobbing as if she knew my grief. Then she turned away and was quiet. "Thank you," I said, somehow confident the cockatoo understood.

When I went to sleep the first night, I cried because I still did not have the strength to sit down on the bed, lift my legs, roll to one side, and fall asleep. I felt I had lost control and that I had done nothing to deserve this. All had been wrenched from me—my daughter, my strength, my mobility, my health. I looked at Bill. "I feel so helpless," I said. "If there's a fire in the house, I can't even get up and run to the door." All this seemed unfair. *Aren't we supposed to be masters of our own destinies? Isn't it true that we are supposed to reap what we sow? Why was it I had done everything right and this was the outcome?*

I knew the answers even as I formed the questions in my feverish brain: Control is an illusion, and, even on our most self-sufficient days, none of us is in control. We are not masters of our own destinies. We do not necessarily reap what we sow. *Deal with it*, I told myself.

The death of Victoria was a situation that could not be changed by any measure of self-delusion, mystical thinking, or force of the will. For the first time, I recognized those things as comforts of human invention and intellect. The realization came as Bill lifted my feet onto the bed. In that moment I was a changed person with a new cosmological clarity, a new definition of self, a new strength. The revelation was a gift from Victoria, or God, or both.

All my adult life I had searched for spiritual meaning, studied metaphysics, immersed myself in the thoughts of great thinkers and their works such as *Summa Theologica* by Thomas Aquinas and *Memories, Dreams and Reflections* by Carl Jung. I had listened to priests and to medicine men. The search had started when I was a very young girl and my parents would take my brother and me on trips to Asia and Europe where we were exposed to many cultures, beliefs, and teachings. That night on the bed, I realized that the greatest teacher is life itself. That thought led me to ponder, *What is life? What is it really?*

The fever passed eventually. I had been home only a couple of days when my doctor asked me to come back to the hospital for an outpatient CAT scan. Two weeks after the stillbirth the scan revealed a pocket of fluid behind my vagina where some of the infection had lodged. I was relieved to get the news but anxious about the painful procedure needed to remove the fluid. Nevertheless, I lay back willingly, feet in stirrups, Bill squeezing my hand, as the doctor inserted a needle and drained the fluid through a syringe. "You're brave," he said. "I couldn't go through this." *I have no choice,* I thought. Soon after that procedure the fever subsided, and I grew better, stronger.

That weekend Bill and I drove to the funeral home to choose an urn for Victoria's ashes, which we wanted with us in the house. We chose a white urn in the shape of a little girl angel kneeling in prayer. *It will be some little body I can hold,* I thought. *Not a warm one with breath, not one that wriggles and reaches up with little fisted hands, but a kind of body.*

A week later when Bill and I returned to the funeral home to pick up the urn, I was happy to run my fingers over its surface. It reminded me of the feel of Victoria's face—smooth and cool. The two of us sat at the funeral director's desk. I held the urn and Bill took out his wallet to pay the bill.

"There will be no charge for the cremation," said the funeral director. "You've been through enough." I looked from the urn to the woman. "I'm so sorry," she added.

Wow, I thought, *something in the world paused because Victoria died. Commerce stopped here at the funeral parlor. What an acknowledgment of my daughter's life.* I had been a little surprised that everything around me had just kept on going even though Victoria had died. Traffic went on and businesses opened and closed and meals were prepared and eaten. She seemed important enough to me to warrant a pause, a reflection. "Thank you," I said to the funeral director. "Thank you," Bill said. And we meant it. All the way home we marveled at the kindness of a stranger.

A few people visited in those early days. My mother stayed with us to clean the house, answer the phone, and keep me company. Aunts visited. My friend Lisa did, too. "I was scared," she told me. "It was the first time I saw you at a loss for words, Lorraine. It's not like you to have nothing to say." It was true. Before I could begin to understand life I had to be rendered speechless and start again.

During my first week home the bereavement counselor called to invite me to the hospital support group for parents who had lost children before birth. Bill opted not to go because he was less inclined to open his inner life to strangers, but I went. There, at least, I discovered other people who shared the same fate and were just as stunned and bewildered. I learned there were other women whose children had died and who also were afraid of losing their husbands. Once Bill had left the hospital room to get some fast food. He was delayed in traffic on the way back and had only been gone for an hour or so, but I was panicked and convinced he had been killed in an accident. Why? I knew anything could happen in an instant, even horrible senseless things, and I knew they could happen to us. The women in the support group understood that.

I learned in that group that men and women can grieve very differently. One man sat quietly next to his wife and held her hand. Another sat quietly with one arm around his wife's shoulders. The women wept and lamented and shared their stories until some outwardly stated they were angry at their husbands. "Don't you care?" one woman said, turning to her man. "Why are you so cold?"

To my eyes, the men were not cold, though. They looked helpless. They were looking for strength in their silence. Although Bill did not attend these sessions they helped solidify my natural feeling that he was grieving, too, but on a different timetable, in a different way. Grief has many faces.

I also learned in that support group there are some stillbirth parents whose anger lights like a struck match at any innuendo that they have been chosen to educate others. They did not want to be lights among the blissfully ignorant majority of people for whom having children is an easy part of life. *I am not one of them*, I thought, *but I cannot blame them.*

In those first few weeks faith helped me—knowing that there is a God. I have been told a hundred times that "God works in mysterious ways," that all is for the best. For some good people, I suppose that perspective is enough. I needed to take it all deeper than that, though. The night after my doctor had drained the last of the infection from my body, I soaked in a hot bath, comforted by the strains of my husband's piano music wafting through our home. *I feel safe, at last.* A songwriter and musician, Bill always composed music on the piano. He was working on an instrumental song, *When You're Gone*. He said it was about loss and that he had started it years earlier but had never finished. "Now I know much more about loss," he said. My understanding grew, too.

CHAPTER SIX

❁

I Am Not Alone

*D*aily I probed, pondered, and dissected what had happened and why it had happened. Over time, the probing started to grow to include all the thinkers, philosophers, and poets I had ever studied—and more. During my eight weeks of recovery at home, I cracked open old texts I had read before. I picked up my beloved *Victorian Poetry and Prose,* a book from a college literature class. Alfred Lord Tennyson's *In Memoriam,* written upon the death of his friend, spoke to me. Tennyson felt "spiritually lacerated" when he wrote the poem, according to the book. Arthur Hallam's death left "his devoted friend stricken with grief and increasingly distressed by doubts as to the beneficence of a God that could sanction the death of so remarkable a man on the very threshold of a great career." I related. I read on, and there was the gem I had been seeking buried in part XXVII:

I envy not in any moods
The captive void of noble rage,
The linnet born within the cage,
That never knew the summer woods;

I envy not the beast that takes
His license in the field of time,
Unfetter'd by the sense of crime,
To whom a conscience never wakes;

Nor, what may count itself as blest,
The heart that never plighted troth
But stagnates in the weeds of sloth;
Nor any want-begotten rest.

I hold it true, whate'er befall;
I feel it, when I sorrow most;
'Tis better to have loved and lost
Than never to have loved at all.

It took Tennyson eighteen years to write that. It took me forty to understand it. How many times had I read it before? Everything I read after the loss of Victoria seemed imbued with new meaning. I started "getting" things I had missed and I longed to read an account of a woman who had gone down the path I was traveling, to know how she faced stillbirth in every detail. I wanted to know how she felt, how long it took to feel better, what made her feel better. I wanted to know and to know and to know.

What I found was different. There were good booklets with titles like *When Hello Means Goodbye* and *Newborn Death* and good books about grief written by therapists sitting with a patient on one side of them and a textbook on the other. What was best about the grief books were the snippets of firsthand accounts from mothers, but they were fleeting. I wanted a lot more. I figured that so few women go through such tragedy that there was little demand for such a story, and that made me feel lonely. That made me feel worse. Frankly, that made me feel even more of a failure.

Maybe I had done something wrong, I thought, and for awhile I considered that possibility. As always, my father had tried to help. He told me even if there was something I had done, which there was not, I would have done it unwittingly. That was true and logical, even right. Still, it was a reality, a plain and simple emotional fact that having a stillborn child made me feel like an inadequate woman. No, the feeling did not overwhelm me, but it was one I needed to beat into submission. While it was true that I had not done anything, even remotely, to bring harm to Victoria, it was indeed my body that had failed. My body had betrayed me and Victoria. Did it not?

The fact that 99 percent of the writings about mothering and birthing were written about success stories only punctuated my sudden depression. Other women were blossoming flowers of pregnancy. They were beautiful and returned from the hospital with little darlings and tales of how the Bradley or Lamaze method had worked for them, how they had not needed drugs, how beautiful it all was, or what a euphoric hormonal high they had been on. Meanwhile, my uterus, infected and hot, had been too tired to work at all. Pitocin had not been able to jump-start it for labor. What the hell was that about? *What made me different from these other models of motherhood?* I asked myself. *We looked the same going in, didn't we? Why hadn't we come out the same?*

Yes, it was nice to find out through the Wisconsin Stillbirth Service Program that there is a 97 percent chance that future pregnancies of women in my situation do not end in stillbirth. It is even life-affirming and wonderful to know that. But, I asked myself, *What does that have to do with grieving the baby already lost?*

During the first months after the stillbirth I lived mentally in the future some of the time. In those days I felt sure that whoever had devised the phrase "live in the present" was a lunatic. I thought, *Whoever it was could not possibly have experienced this pain, a kind that makes the present simply intolerable.* Living in the present was bad advice. It took me four months to open the little pink-flowered bag I had packed to bring into the delivery room. One day, suddenly and inexplicably, I wanted to touch what was inside the bag. As I took out each thing, I relived in a surreal way what I once had thought the birth of Victoria would be like. There were the tools—the lotion, the vaseline lip gloss, the wooden back massager, lollipops. My Lamaze focal point of concentration was a bear carved of stone, a dainty strap of leather tied under his belly and around his back to hold in place a silver feather and a red hawk. It was a talisman my friend Brian, a Cherokee, had given to me. He explained that in his culture the bear was given to pregnant women for protection and for a safe and easy birth. I placed the bear in a drawer in the nursery, atop Victoria's newborn undershirts, right next to her first pair of shoes—for protection. That was a good memory, getting that bear.

Then it occurred to me, *The pregnancy itself was one long, good memory. Why not honor it?* I tried to hold onto that thought as time passed. But nonetheless, I wanted to know how many families were suffering what Bill and I suffered. I wanted to know, *Does this actually happen in the United States of America to perfectly healthy, conscientious, clean-living women?*

My journalistic acumen stepped in and I began to research. I was prepared to find out the truth—even if what had happened to my Victoria was one in a million and that was the reason why no mother had written about stillbirth. I was wrong. Way wrong. During my research I did find a few books by mothers of stillborn babies—one by a mother who had gone through six stillbirths, a fact I did not find inspirational. There was another book reviewed by other stillbirth mothers disgusted by its insensitivity, so I passed on that one. I found a collection of accounts that featured short stories by mothers of stillborns, mothers who had miscarried, and women who had chosen to abort. I also found tons of poetry books comprising odes to specific dead babies. I was moved by them, one and all. Friends gave me grief books, too, but not one helped me move forward through my emotions into recovery.

I looked into feminist writings. I thought, *Surely a movement that has written so profoundly and prolifically about women's lives would cover stillbirth.* Feminist writings helped me through my life before the stillbirth and no doubt will help me through menopause with their volumes about wise women. But motherhood is a troublesome topic, usually written about in terms of its politics, in terms of abortion and day care. When it came to this special brand of female grief, I found nothing.

On the Internet I found that religious women, as a group, dealt better with grief and I felt I had hit gold when I found the organization "Mommies Enduring Neonatal Death," or MEND, based in Coppell, Texas and headed by Rebekah Mitchell, its founder and president. She produced a newsletter for grieving mothers. What a great deal of good she has brought into the world by making her newsletter available at no cost to women such as me. Quickly I came to love her.

I also discovered during my Internet quest that Canadian and Australian women have a lot more organized support around stillbirth than American women. Again, I thought, *This must be because American women so rarely experience stillbirth.* After all, my edition of the classic *What to Expect When You're Expecting* makes only one reference to stillbirth in all of its 437 pages. My assumption about Americans and stillbirth was wrong. What I found in my journalistic forays into the topic astonished me.

There were one million fetal losses in the United States in 1999, according to the National Center for Health Statistics. Twenty-six thousand of those losses— the equivalent of seventy-one babies a day—were stillbirths, meaning the babies died after the twentieth week in utero. Nearly one in two hundred unaborted pregnancies in the United States will end in stillbirth annually, according to statistics from The National Institute of Child Health & Human Development.

The numbers add up to this: There are a lot of mothers going through one of the most profound griefs that can assault the human spirit. Consider, too, all the fathers, siblings, extended family members, and friends who are grief-stricken by these perinatal losses. I came to know this group as the "invisible society." The sheer number of people in my life affected by Victoria's death became apparent to me when I returned home and then to work.

My first day back at work I went to the Irish deli down the street from the newspaper office to grab a sandwich. Ed, the deli owner, greeted me with a smile. "Darlin'," he said, "nice to see you back. How's your baby?"

"Well, Ed," I said. "She died." His face fell. He looked down at the roll of bologna he had been carrying to the slicing machine. "She was stillborn, Ed. An infection." As I spoke, tears welled. I recognized the darkness that dimmed the light in Ed's eyes. "I've been down that road," he said. "My first child was stillborn. I'm so sorry, darlin'."

The invisible society continued to reveal itself in the months after Victoria's death. My neighbor offered to talk; she had lost her second baby to stillbirth. Then there was the woman down the street. She had lost a baby, too, and dealt with her grief by volunteering as a counselor to help other women. My mother revealed my aunt, the mother of two grown children, had lost a baby in utero at eight months. No one had ever before mentioned a word.

When a woman from California called the newspaper to offer me stories from an electronic story service, she asked about my new arrival. "Oh no," she murmured when she heard my answer. After a brief silence, she said, "I lost my first four children to stillbirth."

A colleague, an old, tried and true source for the women's issues column I had written for several years, asked after Victoria. I told her. "Oh, fuck!" she yelled into the phone in what I have to admit was one of the most satisfying responses. "That happened to me, too. My second baby." On it went. As I shared my story of stillbirth I went from feeling alone to feeling I could fill ten baseball stadiums with mothers like me. So why is nothing written? I feel I know. No one knows what to say: Not the mothers who have gone through stillbirth and not the people who know those mothers. People fumble for something, anything to make things better.

My mother-in-law, whose second child died at delivery due to placenta previa, offered a thought. "The death of a child," she said, "is so against the tide of nature that people are shocked into silence." She also explained that her stillbirth experience had not been at all like mine. In her childbearing years during the 1950s, she was not given the option of even seeing her little Maggie after she died. Technology was such that she could not even have known beforehand if Maggie was a girl or that Maggie was healthy.

I knew Victoria was a girl and that she was healthy. I talked to her during my pregnancy. I bought dresses for Victoria. We had more of a prenatal relationship than was possible for my mother-in-law and her unborn daughter. I had pursued and built on that relationship with fervor during the pregnancy. The same technology that allowed me to know Victoria also reassured me all along the way, with test after test, that she was healthy. Passing all those medical tests with flying colors lulled me into a false sense of security about Victoria's safe arrival. Never did it enter my mind that she would not make it. Never did any woman with whom I took my Lamaze class let fall such a fear. I fell in love with Victoria. They fell in love with their darlings. My relationship, all our relationships, were at full throttle before the births.

During my first weeks back at the newspaper I covered a story about Huguenot Street in New Paltz, New York, billed as one of the oldest streets in the United States. The church graveyard dating to the early 1700s is filled with headstones for children. The guide said the infant mortality rate in that time and place was 40 percent. During that assignment I learned that many colonial

American families had between twenty and thirty children because it was common for a dozen of them to die young. Anna and Robert Francoeur write in *Hot and Cool Sex* that in mid-Victorian England the average mother gave birth to six live children. I wondered if those women allowed themselves to bond with unborn children given the high mortality rate at birth.

Tales of individual women's lives from eras gone by seem impossible to me. Queen Anne, who ruled England from 1702 to 1714, birthed thirteen children. All but one, the Duke of Gloucester, died in childhood. The duke reached eleven. *How did Queen Anne go on living?* I wondered. *Surely Queen Anne and I started our pregnancies with different expectations and concomitantly different degrees of closeness to our unborn children,* I told myself.

In this era women do not anticipate the baby's death, so they bond with their unborn children. We do talk about the medical reasons pregnancies are lost, but why isn't there more writing from mothers who endure this grief? Mothers like me do not know what to do with their love. Mothers whose babies are warm and snuggly in their arms usually know how to care for their children. But I could not find answers to the question: How do I love Victoria, whose ashes are in a white angel-shaped urn on her changing table, set there as if it were a shrine?

When I was pregnant I found a way to love my daughter, here in the physical world, when I started a diary about the two of us. It is small and contains snatches of phrases and thoughts and images. I jotted down snippets of conversation about her. At the time I started my pregnancy journal, I could not have known it would become my only tangible way to continue our relationship. When I came home from the hospital without Victoria, I continued to write in it until I began this book. My diary became the story of our ongoing love. On June 24, three weeks after I delivered Victoria, I wrote:

While walking today, I got to thinking my precious Victoria perhaps will live not in an eternal night but in an eternal morning, in a place where the sun is always shining, where good is as clear as a clean spring sky, where God is caring for her even though her mother cannot, where all the possibilities are good and where—I pray most fervently—she can see and know and understand that her earthly parents miss and love her even as they live in a place where night falls, where what is good is sometimes hard to see and where sometimes the view of heaven is so clouded we wonder if it is there at all. But I believe it is. I hope it is. I hope it is the place my baby girl calls home.

CHAPTER SEVEN

✿

The Question of God and the Great Beyond

*T*here is solace in thinking of Victoria as being with God, but the problem with heaven at times like this is that it seems so very far away.

I wrote a newspaper column in which I mentioned Victoria's passing in two short paragraphs to illustrate a larger point about the ravages of nature. A reader wrote me a note: "I do pray that you will be comforted by knowing that this precious little person is already in her heavenly home, fully alive, fully rejoicing."

One of my doctors told me, "Your daughter is in a better place now. This is such a crazy world."

My sister-in-law who had miscarried a child two years before Victoria's delivery, gave me a statuette of a sleeping baby with an inscription that reads "Safe in the Arms of Jesus." There is a loveliness to that, a soothing sweetness like the taste of a spiritual peach, and yet there is an underside to the sentiment, too.

Love demands connection. I once read an edition of *Parabola* magazine devoted to the idea that all sadness is a kind of separation. There is no separation as final as death. That Victoria's death followed the most intensely close physical connection possible between two people made it all the more painful.

So many people trying to comfort me blamed God for Victoria's death. A hundred times I heard, "God had His reasons." They were stating the unspoken assumption that God "took" my child. Some were saying, "God took Victoria before her time," and others were saying, "Nine-and-a-half months was Victoria's time, as decreed in heaven." Still, others had a different take on it, although God was still their central focus. "I don't see how there could be a God," Christine said, her lip quivering, "because if there were a God, He wouldn't let this happen."

I could not allow myself to ponder what God was thinking, but I started from a place of trust—a lifetime steeped in Catholicism, which I often challenged but nevertheless always honored. I simply believed what Saint Augustine said in the fourth century: Faith precedes understanding. I simply believed the Jesuit theologian Teilhard de Chardin when he wrote in *Le Milieu Divin*, "If we believe, then, everything is illuminated and takes shape around us: chance is seen to be order, success assumes an incorruptible plenitude, suffering becomes a visit and caress of God."

These age-old luminaries were helping me through my grief. Instinctively, I believed what they wrote. I did not know, of course, whether they were right. *Such things are unknowable*, I told myself, *and human tragedy does nothing to lift the veil of mystery between heaven and earth.* But it did me good to contemplate my beliefs. In that contemplation lay one of the greatest gifts my daughter's life brought to me— a clearer view of God's role in the natural order of things. I came to a view of life and myself that seemed to explain how terrible things like Victoria's stillbirth could happen in God's creation.

Did God—He, She, or It—rule that Victoria should die? If the answer is, *Yes,* how could I turn to God for comfort? How could I revere the same being who would kill my daughter? For me, the answer is, *No, God did not rule that Victoria should die.*

I began carefully thinking about who God is as opposed to what nature is. Harold Kushner helped me with that. A Massachusetts rabbi whose son, Aaron, died at the age of fourteen from progeria, or rapid aging, Kushner wrote the renowned book, *When Bad Things Happen to Good People.* As soon as my painkiller was reduced enough to allow me to concentrate, I began reading Kushner's book every night. Rabbi Kushner wrote his book to help others through tough times. His example, in part, drove me to write my own story as a way to transmute something painful into something helpful.

Desperately, I wanted to imbue Victoria's existence with meaning and that search had to include an answer to the question, *What had killed her?* In the course of my reading, slowly I chose to give up the belief that God was all-powerful. Instead, I chose to believe God was hard put to stop the death of Victoria, a pure and innocent soul.

What, then, were Victoria and I and God powerless against? Could it be nature? Granted, God created nature, but the nature He created is inherently unpredictable and hardly benign.

Nature is ruled by laws implicit with danger. Take gravity, for example. Gravity is a good thing. It ensures that everything on earth stays down in its place. However, as Kushner explained:

> *Gravity makes objects fall. Sometimes they fall on people and hurt them. Sometimes gravity makes people fall off mountains and out of windows. Sometimes gravity makes people slip on ice or sink under water. We could not live without gravity, but that means we have to live with the dangers it causes. Laws of nature treat everyone alike.*

One of the first good laughs I had after Victoria's death was while reading Kushner's book. I imagined God as an old rabbi in the sky throwing up both his hands, "What? I have a whole world here to make go. You could do better?" I relaxed after that. I had found a rational way to support my belief in God. I had found a way to be angry at what happened to me without being angry at God.

My attention engaged more completely on these matters when I went off the painkiller, roughly a month after the stillbirth. New thoughts and the kindnesses of friends and family started to weave themselves into a cloak of healing. By that time I had just enough fabric sewn to feel its texture. I took in Kushner's idea that perhaps we humans should not regard nature, or indeed the creation of the world as we know it, as a done deal. As we walk down the street, conceive a child, read a book, grow food, or prepare a pan of lasagna, all about us seems set in concrete, somehow finished. When something goes wrong, we perceive it as an error, regard it as something that should not have happened.

Yet maybe, Kushner wrote, the world is not finished. Our evolutions as individuals and as societies suggest that to us every day. The notion never had occurred to me. Not in just this way. Using the Biblical metaphor of the six days of Creation, Kushner suggests, "Maybe it is only Friday afternoon." No sooner had my eyes read those words than I felt God holding my hand. I put down the book. It took several days of walking up and down my street and looking at trees and into the sky before this truth sunk in. *It is only Friday afternoon,* I told myself, *and the fever that killed Victoria was an act of nature that is inherently unpredictable and still evolving.*

A few weeks later I was talking to a friend about nature and about God, and she said casually, "Yes, the infection was an act of nature. But infections are nasty to fetuses; they do bad things to the brain. So maybe her death was an act of God." The possibility dawned that perhaps Victoria's death had been an act of God's mercy. Who could say what she would have been like if she had survived the ordeal? How much pain would she have felt? How much potential would she have lost? I did not know.

As I continued to ask these questions, I reassured myself again, *These things are unknowable.* But I did know this: In a couple of months I already had come a very long way from being the shocked and speechless woman in the hospital room at the end of the maternity ward.

Understanding that God was not personally to blame for Victoria's death was a powerful reaffirmation of faith. Even more central to my belief and healing was another fundamental tenet of faith that involved my very connection to Victoria—eternal life. There had been times in my life when I accepted eternal life, and times when I had not believed a word.

Faced with Victoria's stillbirth, I asked myself, *Now what do I believe?* Any talk of eternity first brings thoughts of heaven. The presentation of paradise as a place of all-consuming bliss somewhere over the rainbow made me feel lousy. John O'Donohue's *Anam Cara*, a book of Celtic wisdom, contains a gem that made me feel better:

> *The dead are our nearest neighbors; they are all around us. Meister Eckhart was once asked, Where does the soul of a person go when the person dies? He said, no place. Where else would the soul be going? Where else is the eternal world? It can be nowhere other than here. We have falsely spatialized the eternal world. We have driven the eternal out into some kind of distant galaxy. Yet the eternal world does not seem to be a place but rather a different state of being. The soul of the person goes no place because there is no place else to go. This suggests that the dead are here with us, in the air that we are moving through all the time. The*

only difference between us and the dead is that they are now in an invisible form. You cannot see them with the human eye. But you can sense the presence of those you love who have died. With the refinement of your soul, you can sense them. You feel that they are near.

I wondered, *Could it be that Victoria is in the air I move through all the time?* My mind churned with these thoughts and settled momentarily on the notion Victoria was in the same room with me. I loved that idea and believed it in a moment. I have felt the presence of my grandfather around me so vividly at various points in my life that I could almost smell him, almost hear his laugh.

Soon, though, I needed to move beyond the idea Victoria was near. I was plagued by and absolutely transfixed with the notion she had passed on without knowing she had two loving, grieving parents on earth who missed her so much they were practically bleeding from their souls. Then one day—it was June 29—I was online and darting around looking for websites on perinatal loss. Up like a little miracle popped an AOL buddy, a Cherokee medicine woman I had come to know through a mutual friend. She had made a miniature cradleboard for Victoria. The message chimed up, "Hi, sweetie."

We spoke. "MomFeather," I asked, "does Victoria know that she has two grieving parents who hold her in their hearts?"

"Yes ma'am," came the reply. "She does know and she knows also that she can give you the strength you need.

When you are ready for another child she will be very close to you for protection."

"How can I speak to her?" I asked.

"If you listen carefully you will know she is but a breath away—the things that you will hear, dear, come within you. This is the place where good things start."

"But a breath away." *Just one breath*. Here was someone suggesting I could communicate with Victoria. The whisper of inner voices was not foreign to me. What writer has not heard them? Also, I had meditated for years. *I'll listen*, I thought. *I'll listen hard*.

I got to thinking about the movie *Field of Dreams*, in which the hero, a farmer, hears a voice that tells him, "If you build it, he will come." The first half of the movie consists of the man figuring out that "it" is a baseball field, and the end reveals who "he" is—the ghost of the man's father. *All right*, I thought, *I'll work on my own version of that. I'll call it "If you listen, she will speak."* Victoria speaks, and Victoria continues to speak.

MomFeather had given me a little peace, just an opening. I latched onto it and it grew. I thought, *This is how I will build a recovery—thought by thought*. My ideas about heaven and the afterlife had changed and so had I. After all, don't we become what we think about, and doesn't what we think about grow? When our ideas change, as Proust said, we see with different eyes. So it was with different eyes I was looking for Victoria, with different ears that I was listening for her all around me, and my sense of separation eased, so much so that it seemed she had never left. In a way, she had not.

I said goodbye and let Victoria go, but she seemed still as much a part of me as when she was within me. Just as any pregnant woman can sense the moods and feelings of her child within, so I could still sense the moods and feelings of Victoria entering my consciousness. She was somehow woven into my thought streams and emotional life. Not that I need her to be there, but I find her there most always. Her presence may not be by my choice, but it certainly is the great blessing of my life.

If love from one dimension can permeate the next, there is a continuity of lives between here and beyond. My every instinct tells me my love reaches Victoria in the world in which she exists. I believe in eternity now.

CHAPTER EIGHT

✦

Divine Silence

*I*n the month before Victoria was born, I did something that, when looked at in retrospect, truly helped focus my spiritual lens: I went to a psychic.

After the nursery had been set up, the last vaginal bacterial test passed, and the house cleaned, I got to the niceties. I said to my husband, "I'd like to get a reading on Victoria. Wouldn't that be nice?" "Nice" is the best word I can use to describe the feeling. It is vaguely positive, which summed up my sentiments toward psychic endeavors regarding Victoria or otherwise. So off we went and, oh, what a reading Bill and I got that day.

According to the reading, Victoria would be the embodiment of his best qualities and mine. She would be kind and smart, loving and responsible, a tad overly serious like her mother used to be. Her intelligence would span many fields, like that of her father.

My husband and I had joked throughout the pregnancy as we speculated what Victoria might be like. I had often quoted Abraham Lincoln's probably apocryphal response to a young, beautiful woman who was infatuated with him. "Oh, Abe," she said, doting on him, "let's marry and have children. Think of it. They could have my looks and your brains." To which the would-be president replied, "Yes, but suppose they have my looks and your brains?"

While driving to the reading, Bill and I talked, yet again, about what it is that psychics read. Were they reading minds and regurgitating what already existed in their clients' thoughts? When they spoke of past lives, were they picking up on what he called "sympathetic resonances," themes in the current lives of their clients recast in different eras and places? Who knew? These things, too, were unknowable. But I had always harbored a small spot of respect for real clairvoyant talent.

As a journalist, I can ask a mean tough question. In fact, I ask lots of questions. And that day I did ask: Would the delivery be early or late? Smooth or difficult? Natural or C-section? The psychic's answers came easily: "A little late. Smooth. Natural."

Sure enough, the delivery was a little late, but it was hell and it was surgery. What had happened? How could this psychic be so off? How could her reading be so horrendous? The experience cured me of all illusions.

If God has relinquished control over nature and does not control the course of events, then how could it ever be possible for a mere mortal to foresee what will happen? I decided, *Since we are not even masters of our own destinies, we cannot possibly be able to foretell the destinies of others.*

The best psychics deal in probabilities, in projecting what could happen given current circumstances. In my opinion, that is about as far as it goes. The larger question that presented itself through my experience, though, is more interesting: Why do people pursue psychics at all? Why do people cling to religious doctrines with superhuman zeal? Why do they believe in the superiority of *their* religion, *their* way, *their* truth, as opposed to those of others? We all want answers, that's why. We all want the feeling of safety that answers bring.

Many human endeavors, including my own prior to my relationship with Victoria, followed this pattern. Life presented questions. In some areas, I got satisfying answers. Where I found a satisfying answer, I stopped looking and pursued other questions, following them as if they were a trail that would lead to some electrifying, sensational destination. Many will become convinced along life's paths that they have arrived at the pinnacle of knowledge, and they will stop searching. When they do, they enter ignorance. After all, wisdom is in large part a recognition of how little we know.

For me, if there is anything that an event as momentous, sad, and tragic as a stillbirth will teach, it is that wisdom lies in the asking of questions and delving into one question after another to higher and higher plateaus of understanding. The purpose is not to find an answer and stop; I know beyond a doubt that any answer is a lie, a fabrication, a betrayal, no matter how well-meaning, of humanity. Fully, I understand the expression, "If you see Buddha, run."

In the days of early recovery all this growth was happening in the silence of my inner sanctum. During that time serendipity had led me to find the work of James P. Carse, a professor of the history and literature of religion at New York University. He made a set of audiotapes, *The Silence of God: Prayer, Longing, and the Divine Response*, which I ordered. One day I had been ironing for hours, discouraged because my belly, even months after the C-section, still was a bloated, unfamiliar size. I also was depressed that my body was cruel enough to keep producing milk for a child who did not exist. That was the same day the tapes arrived in the mail.

I ripped open their plastic cover and popped them into the new boombox my husband and I had bought to bring into the delivery room. We had selected many tapes and CDs to play during the birth, but all we had ever listened to was the soft hum of James Taylor songs, and some jazz, in the hospital room. The machine meant to help me mentally bring Victoria into the world was now spewing lectures about grief.

In my support group the topic of God's silence had come up many times. *What does it mean?* the people there wanted to know. I wanted to know, too. What does it mean when you pray and you do not hear anything back? I never participated much in that group conversation because it seemed to me most people really expected to hear a booming paternal voice from the sky. Instead, I was listening to the wind in the trees, to thoughts that floated like clouds through my mind. I was listening closely, as MomFeather had suggested. I was hearing things and I wondered if what I heard was merely my own echo, my own wish to be heard.

James Carse's words rang true for me. Yes, I was listening to myself, he seemed to say, and that was the point. When we speak, he said, we say what the other person, the listener, enables us to say. "Some listeners (therapists, friends)," he goes on, "are so good that we find we are saying things that not only surprise us but actually in some ways transform us. We are transformed, or recreated." He concludes that God is the ultimate listener who "listens in a way that is deeply, profoundly, endlessly creative."

I came to recognize these divine silences as links to the great beyond. Any heavenly listener then—be it God, be it an angel, be it Victoria, or an ancestor—makes it possible for me to be a person I would not have been otherwise. The divine silence is the space for me to find and recreate myself continuously.

I was standing at the window overlooking my backyard and taking in the trees and the creek as Carse stopped speaking and the tape snapped off. For the first time, Victoria's spiritual self felt like a gift. A gift I had not wanted, but a gift. For a long while I stared out the window thinking about nature and its relentless cycles and my milking breasts. Nature killed my baby. The same nature eventually would return me to my usual size, and it would stop my milk from flowing. The same nature would make another baby possible.

Nature had not let me down, for nature itself is nothing more than the potential for something to happen. It is not a guarantee of anything, as I had thought only a year earlier before Victoria had been conceived. I thought, *Now I have no choice but to take life as it comes to me, just as it is with love.* In the most tangled and difficult and unlikely situations, we find unconditional love. In this horrid situation I had found it, too.

Yet, I did not want a heavenly listener. I wanted a daughter to take walks with, a little girl whose hair I could brush and braid. I wanted to hear her sing nursery rhymes and then Broadway tunes and, who knows, maybe arias. I wanted to watch as Victoria discovered herself and to shop with her on Saturday afternoons. I wanted to take her on the trip my mother and I took to Cape May every spring, and to see her blossom into a woman and find a man as wonderful as her father.

No, I did not want a heavenly listener, but that was what I was given. If Victoria and I could have a mystical bond, that is what I would take. I was reminded of what Dostoyevsky wrote in *The Brothers Karamazov*:

> *Much on earth is hidden from us, but to make up for that we have been given a precious mystic sense of our living bond with the other world, with the higher*

heavenly world, and the roots of our thoughts and feelings are not here but in other worlds.

The more I healed, the more fired up I became about accepting the gift I was given. I would stop pining about the stillbirth or regretting it. In the end, I decided, there is only taking life as it comes and learning to love my own fate. It is the only one I have.

CHAPTER NINE

❀

Insensitive People and Extraordinary Kindness

There are three common responses from people who hear my daughter died in stillbirth. One is "I'm sorry." I respond, "Thank you." The second response is stone cold silence and a quick end to the conversation as the other person, nonplussed, turns away. The third response is a fast change of topic. A man I met while out on my beat covering a story asked, "Do you have any children?" I responded, "Yes, I have a daughter who died." Then came the predictable staccato moment. Panic filled his eyes before he answered, "Hey, how about those Yankees?" referring to the World Series. It is the third response that astounds me every time.

Those very few people who ask what happened generally have two questions that betray the pervasive attitude of American culture to stillbirth: "Was she full term?" and "Did you name it?"

Stillbirth mothers who lost their babies at six or eight months sometimes lie and say they went full term because people validate grieving a fully formed baby more readily than one who was less developed. As to asking whether "it" had a name, well, most of our babies do. To stillbirth parents, no baby is an "it"—they are daughters and sons.

Over time I learned how to field all those reactions. I read *The Four Agreements*, the popular book by best-selling Toltec writer Don Miguel Ruiz, whom I interviewed for a newspaper story. The book is about four agreements an individual can make with herself. The second one liberated me from the tyranny of other people's reactions: *Don't take anything personally.* "Nothing people do is because of you," Ruiz writes. "It is because of themselves. All people live in their own dream, in their own mind; they are in a completely different world from the one (you) live in."

Most surprising to me, though, was that the world of mothers blessed with live, healthy children seemed the farthest away from my world. Those in my close circle of friends were supportive and helpful to me, but the minute I stepped out of that small secure circle, trouble was ahead. The other moms in my perinatal loss support group noticed the same thing—there was something about us mothers of dead fetuses and babies that brought out the worst in our more fortunate counterparts.

These women fell in two groups. In one group were the pregnant mothers who simply would not look at me. Around them I felt like bad luck with legs, someone with a visible curse hanging over her head. I was a downer to be avoided. One woman in my Lamaze class whom I had gotten to know also was expecting a girl; we shared the same due date and we had made promises to meet and walk our daughters together. Before our babies were born, we had kept up with one another on the phone: "How are you feeling today?" "Heavy! And you?" I was surprised when, after traveling so much shared terrain with this woman, she simply never called back after I informed her of Victoria's death. I had been erased, deleted.

Pregnant women, I soon learned, could not wait to end a conversation with me. I embodied their worst nightmare. They wanted to push me and my daughter out of their consciousness and leave room for only positive, good things. I understood. For them, my experience was the equivalent of negative thinking. When I was pregnant I focused mainly on a good outcome, too. At the beginning of the fourth month I remarked to my husband that I felt safe because I had made it successfully through the first trimester. At the beginning of the ninth month, one friend, who knew that my cousin's daughter had died after living only days and that my sister-in-law had miscarried her child, called to reassure me. "Nothing like that will happen to you," she said. I thanked her, but thought, *How do you know?*

Even while hoping for the best I did not shield myself from stories of the worst when I was pregnant. I did not invite any tales of horror but neither did I walk away when they were offered. I listened for three reasons. First, I wanted to learn from others' experiences and thought pieces of their stories might help me on my journey. Second, I was amazed at the diversity of childbirth experiences in the world. Third, as a writer, I am a professional listener. For twenty years I had searched for the facts, however harsh, on countless subjects. I knew life was filled with unhappy endings.

Two years before I became pregnant, when I was an editor at the newspaper, I had assigned a story about stillbirth to a reporter. When I spoke to one of the stillbirth mothers included in that story, I listened carefully and asked her many questions about what had happened to her and her baby. I did not want to be shielded from the experience. Perhaps it was easy for me to listen then because, though I felt compassion for the woman, I also felt a degree of removal not only from stillbirth but from all issues involving childbirth. It was as though there were a sheet of glass between her life and mine. I could reach out to her and talk but I could not truly touch her, not really understand how her heart had been wrenched.

Getting pregnant still was a deferred dream then, and picturing myself as a mother was like anticipating some future incarnation of myself. After Victoria died I reflected on the layout I had created for that stillbirth story two years earlier. At the center was a large picture of that sad mother with long hair holding a white urn and looking longingly at it. I thought, *Now I understand you. Now I could touch you.*

I knew stillbirth happened. I did not consider myself immune, but I also felt protected if for no other reason than my pregnancy went superbly well. My mother and I never had a conversation about the possibility of something going wrong but she opposed the baby shower that friends, including my cousin Kathy, planned for me. All her life my mother had opposed the tradition of hosting a baby shower before the birth of a baby. "You never know," she said. "I'm sure everything will go well but you just never know."

The other group of women who did not want to hear about Victoria were new mothers who already had successful births. These women basked in the euphoria of their babies and were more than happy to instruct me in how to achieve such bliss with a future pregnancy and birth. "Surely the *next* time you will get it right," one new mother confidently told me. I listened to many happy stories about the joys of natural childbirth. These moms would go on and on about what they believed is their superior knowledge of their own anatomies. Knowledge is power, they said. Know your body, they said. "Take back your power from the medical profession," one woman declared, "and all will be well." They seemed to imply I did not know my vagina from my uterus.

One woman attributed my stillbirth to the fact I had a male doctor, who, of course, had never given birth and therefore was not competent to grasp the situation. By the time I reached this piece of haughty advice, I had had enough. "My father's cancer specialist never had cancer," I replied, "and yet my father has been alive and well in the twenty-two years since the operation on his colon."

"Well, I certainly hope you're going to sue your doctor," one mother said to me. "This is inexcusable." No matter that she did not know any of the medical facts of the case.

"Maia had her baby and her baby was just fine," my masseuse said one day. "She said she didn't have any problem because her doctor thought to do a bacterial test." My response was swift: "So did mine."

One friend angry with my unstable emotions wrote she suspected I was jealous of her because her children were alive while I had suffered a stillbirth and nearly died in the process.

Someone suggested to me that if I killed myself I could be with my daughter and ease my pain. I was told to be happy with whatever solace I could sew together from fragments of time others could give me. I was told my intensity and grief were in bad taste.

As if babies were interchangeable, I was told not to worry about the stillbirth because certainly I would have another baby and, if I did not, I would adopt one. For the first time I understood a story my father once had told me. The child of a colleague had died and my father, then a young man, went to the funeral. In an effort to soothe his colleague, he had said, "At least you have nine more children."

The bereaved father replied, "I have ten fingers, too, and I want each one."

Once when I said I had pictures of Victoria, I got this reply: "Don't show me any pictures of your baby. My stomach couldn't take it." I said, "Of course, I understand."

Then, when I walked away, I got angry. *Now wait a minute*, I thought, *why am I consoling her? Why am I being so understanding? What possessed her to think that any mother in the universe would want to hear that pictures of her baby would make someone ill?* No matter if the baby is alive or dead, that is about as offensive as a statement gets.

Mothers of stillborn children often wind up soothing others. At least that is my experience and that of many women in my support group. "This is weird," said the mother of Hunter, stillborn at six months. "Why am I cushioning the blow for other people?" It was a fine question. Eventually we parents came to realize that we may be the only firsthand witnesses of life's brutalities that some people know. Talking to us may be as close as many people have ever come to real horror. Perhaps stillbirth moms are all that stand between them and the horror, and they desperately want us to keep silent about what we experienced. No matter how great the need for still-birth moms to testify, most people want us to shield them from the blood and pain. They would rather not know. They are afraid to know. That leaves us parents talking to each other, to others who have known deep loss, and to those of our friends willing to listen.

In these early days I spent a lot of time emailing friends and talking to them on the phone. As was the case throughout my recovery, the majority of people who helped me along were men—my husband, my father, my friends—and a few understanding women, including my mother. I can say that through this sad and difficult time,

I was carried on their kindnesses. Never was I so acutely aware of how much I am dependent on help from family and friends—all offering a special piece of themselves. I had lost Victoria's heartbeat, but with their help I did not let myself lose heart.

On one particularly frustrating day a former professor from graduate school, George, sent an insightful email about what I had been grappling with:

"Remember that, as your friends and relatives visit you, they are probably as stressed—or more stressed—by you than you are by their inability to know what to say, to advise, to do. They feel as guilty as you may now, but their guilt is based on the fact that they have been spared what you went through. Be gentle."

From that point on I went gently. Like the Desiderata in motion, I went quietly amid outrageous comments that often sounded like accusations. People with orderly lives had pat answers—"It's for the best"— or, worse yet, they tried to divert my attention—"Are you going to the arts center this summer?" They did not seem to know that fortune could turn on anyone, including them. I did know.

During this phase of recovery, which lasted several months, a revelation shone on me: When most people talked at me they were really trying to keep intact, in the face of the senseless facts of life, their own fragile views about justice in the universe. They wanted to keep undisturbed their deep-seated optimism that we can all direct our destinies and, even more so, the notion that they themselves are personally safe. My story shook their deepest fears about childbirth and about life.

Most of the people who came in contact with me resisted, and I suppose will continue to resist, the reality of their own vulnerability. I heard so many rationalizations, including "You lost your baby because of bad karma from a past life." Now I believe most of us are slaves to illusion. I said little in response to all this fear because, frankly, I understand it. I have been there. In addition to being a mother grieving the loss of her daughter, I also am a woman grieving the loss of her own naiveté about the cosmos.

But why had that insight about going gently through the emotional minefields come from a male friend and not from a woman who, I used to think, should know the situation better than a man? A couple of weeks after I had returned to work, my friend Brian called me at the office. "When do they let you out of your cage for some lunch?" he asked. An hour later I found myself sitting in a restaurant telling him how ostracized I felt.

"Wow," he said, "inside you must be looking at these people and thinking: 'You're really hurting me but I know you mean well. So I'd really like to put you through the food processor, but I won't.'"

Splendid, I thought. "Yes," I said. "That's what I feel, but why do things work like that?"

That night Brian sent an answer via email: "On men's consolation—the only thing that comes to mind is the awareness that we men can never truly comprehend what it's like to lose a baby that you've carried around inside you, and we know that it can't happen to us. Perhaps another woman feels she would have done things differently, or just wants to distance herself from the possibility."

Perhaps, but after awhile I lost the obsession for wanting other mothers to understand me, to welcome me into their club. I lost the need for acceptance when I started noticing that for every angst-ridden comment thrust at me, there was a beautiful one as well. My uncommon tragedy had unleashed uncommon fears and insecurities, but it also had given rise to uncommon acts of compassion and kindness.

A friend of mine wrote: "All my life, it seems, I have been surrounded by this kind of loss. I don't think there is a worse pain. I have seen how it can twist a woman's soul, and I have seen it melt the walls of a mother's heart, exposing the rarest kind of beauty and grace and compassion."

I found this true. At a luncheon I was seated across from a co-worker who had just had a baby girl. Out came the photos and the oohing and aahing about how cute and beautiful the baby was. The sheer thoughtlessness made me angry, enabling me to hold back tears.

When I returned to my office after that lunch, I found in my mail a card from an old news source. Still stinging from seeing the baby pictures, I opened the envelope to find these words: "My thoughts of you could wear the trail to your door. In grief, a journey can be reduced to just getting through the next moment. I wish you comfort in those moments and support for the special healing you are going through. Take good care of yourself, you are special."

My bond with my mother, an Italian-American woman, all of 4 feet 11 inches and 110 pounds, was especially healing. Continuing a lifelong pattern, she was there for me in the hospital and beyond. Of all my loved ones, she said the least and watched me the most. I knew she had to feel the most. I was her daughter and Victoria, her granddaughter. She had to feel the violence done to the graceful passing of one generation into the next as sharply as I did. There is no doubt after Victoria was wrenched from me, I needed my mommy close by.

A week after the stillbirth my stomach remained a hard painful ball of gas. Specialists suspected that my intestines were not working properly, so they ordered an x-ray from the radiology department, two floors down from my hospital room. Just the thought of getting from the bed to the wheelchair exhausted me. Never mind the thought of traveling two floors, moving from the wheelchair to a table, and standing erect against a machine. Then I would have to get back in the chair, and endure the bumpy ride back to my room. I thought, *I just can't take all that movement. How will I do this?*

The moment I pushed away the bedcovers, exhaustion and cold engulfed me. Shaking and frightened, I let Bill help me into the wheelchair. A small group of visitors concerned for my welfare had gathered outside my door. I looked up and saw my seventy-two-year-old mother standing against the opposite wall of the hallway, pocketbook primly over one forearm, her gaze only for me. When our eyes met, she smiled—a wide, deep, loving smile, the kind of smile da Vinci would paint. Everyone else was conferring, busy with the business of my sickness—except my mother. She looked at me adoringly, as sweetly as if I, her baby, were a newborn in the maternity ward. Even as I tried to smile back, I realized most deeply what I had missed because Victoria could not open her eyes.

When I returned from the x-ray ordeal, my mother was in the room, my father at her side. Memories comforted me as sleep came swiftly. Eyes closed, I envisioned wind-scented sheets and my mother's pursed lips on my feverish forehead. Her very presence always made me feel as precious as a diamond.

In those early days back from the hospital when I was still shell-shocked and hardly interested enough in life to brush my teeth, the company of other women was sweet as well. I was disheartened by my appearance and unaccustomed to being out of shape. Before I got pregnant I was constantly in aerobics and toning classes at a local gym. Now I was fat, winded, and weak. I could summon no physical strength. My hair was graying because I didn't want to color it while pregnant, lest chemicals affect the baby. My feet were swollen and my waist still so thick I could only wear maternity clothes. Once I had happily donned them but now they appeared dowdy and irrelevant.

I wanted to reactivate my enthusiasm for life and decided that improving how I looked would help. I wanted flashy clothes with shine and style. I had my hair colored "chocolate" with a vegetable solution—just in case I got pregnant again, the baby wouldn't be affected by chemical dyes. During a trip to a mall with my mother and her best friend I bought the largest-sized pants and blouses I had ever purchased in my life, but they were classy and colorful—gold, orange, and purple.

In my family, lust for life always was reflected in lots of fresh, healthy cooking. Good food meant nurturing and affection. So it was special to me when Debra, a friend and reporter at the newspaper where I worked, organized a food brigade in the newsroom and delivered to my house enough dinners, fruits, iced teas, cakes, and casseroles to last two weeks. Each dish came with a note signed by whomever had made it. What memories that brigade brought back.

For years my Uncle Primo, a chef trained in Italy, and his wife, Esther, had owned a boarding house in Chester, New York. As a girl I went to huge family get-togethers there. My Aunt Esther, apron still draped over her, would clap her hands together in delight as I walked in the door. "Bella, bella," she would say, cradling my face in her hands, still white from rolling dough. "We have nice pasta and cheese." Then she would kiss my forehead, take my hand and before I knew it I would be in her kitchen and my cousins were all around me. In no time my uncles, in white shirts or overalls, would be playing cards or talking with each other, and the women would be setting out platters and bowls and arranging food. Aromas of homemade sauces and pastas, meats and pastries, and freshly baked loaves of bread wafted through their home as we children set the long tables. Most of the homes in my extended family were just like that.

During those first few weeks after I got home I created a dinner ritual, inspired by comforting family gatherings. I looked forward to sitting in a rocking chair in front of the television in our living room around 6 o'clock. Before me was a tray table, complete with linen place mat, napkin and silverware, and I was ready to eat. Bill would come in and play waiter, reciting the list of options. My favorite became baked ziti, made by a colleague's wife. Eventually I got the recipe and to this day, I affectionately think of the ziti as my favorite comfort food.

Certainly my cousin Kathy, whose daughter had died days after birth, was an enormous comfort during those first months. It was she who knew, before I did, how important it was to have something tangible to remind me of Victoria. So she gave me a delicate gold heart necklace with fancy edges. On the front were two interlocking hearts—one large, one small. I liked holding it tight in the palm of my hand.

When the hospital bereavement counselor called to say she would mail the pictures of Victoria she had taken, I panicked. "No!" I said. "Don't put them in the mail. We'll pick them up." I was terrified those pictures, the only ones we would ever have of Victoria, would be lost. Bill drove me to the hospital where, in the lobby, the counselor placed the photos in my hands.

Immediately I had a favorite one of Victoria's sweet face. One day Bill surprised me with a gold locket etched with a long-stemmed rose on the front. Inside was that very picture and from that day forward for more than a year I wore that locket—right over my heart.

After Victoria's death I appreciated all these small beauties as I never had before. Perhaps I retreated into them to find peace. Perhaps it was easier to reflect on a beautiful detail than a horrifying reality. Either way, my life had stopped to contemplate my beloved in all her complexity and, from that fixed point, by extension, the wondrous complex beauties of creation all around me. No longer did I pass by things on the way to some other destination, always looking beyond to the horizon. After all, where was I to go? The only place that interested me was here, the only moment now.

In those early days Christine, a thirty-five-year-old single who was my friend and Bill's cousin, would call all the time. During one long hot July afternoon, when I was home alone and tearfully musing on what could have been, she unexpectedly dropped by with a quart of Häagen-Dazs vanilla fudge ice cream—the most decadent kind. Never before had I taken such time in the middle of an afternoon to enjoy ice cream. Afternoons had always been for news meetings and interviews and deadlines. That day, though, I became aware that everything I saw and tasted seemed divine—the gold of my new pants, which I looked forward to wearing when I went back to work, the sun as it set in the sky, the cheese on the ziti, the taste of vanilla fudge. They all had new wonder about them. *All of life's details blaze with beauty and we are their witnesses,* I thought, *until at some point they vanish, or we do, in a moment.*

CHAPTER TEN

❀

Re-Entering the World

Slowly I lost weight, but very slowly. Most mornings I would look in the mirror and lament. Nothing was as it had been—not even the look in my eyes, which reflected what they had seen. They reflected sadness now and softness, too. I would stare at myself in the mirror for a long time. Bill would come up from behind and embrace me and kiss my neck.

Though Bill supported me, he had little support. Usually, I would be the one to whom he turned for understanding, discussion, and encouragement, but I was a well of need myself. Later he would say he felt it his duty to respond to my every need, insisting I suffered more because of the physical pain and because, he swore, "You knew Victoria better because you carried her." Still, he was her father and needed acknowledgment of his real grief as well. To my eternal gratitude, three men wrote to him during this time. His boss and college buddy wrote: "There hasn't been an hour—let alone a day—that I have not been thinking of you and Lorraine. If you would like more time off, please let me know. Much love, Steve."

Mark wrote from Illinois declaring his devastation and pledging to meet any need Bill expressed. David, a friend and an editor of mine, wrote from Virginia, stirring Bill deeply. After Bill read the letter, he sat on the edge of the bed where I was resting. "David wrote," Bill shared. Then a look of contentment crossed his face. "To me." Bill kept the letter to himself for a couple of weeks and offered no further comment about it, and that was fine with me.

In the days after its arrival his face was less tense and he fell asleep more easily. Comfort seemed to slowly seep into the edges of his grief. I did not inquire about the letter, thinking of it as a bubble of solace just for him. I did not want to puncture the fragile inner world of healing the letter had created. Eventually, though, I did read it:

> You will receive, of course, a lot of expressions that can't express, that say, "I don't know what to say," and they will, of course, be genuine concerns of affection, care, and love. I hope they don't ignore the pain of the father's loss, for we often forget it is the man's child as well as the woman's and the emotional commitment is as great, though different.

> I don't know you, but I don't think such knowledge would give me the words you need to read and I don't even think I can find someone else's words and I don't know a particular God whose providence includes such inexplicable events which seem to have no cause, no reason, no help, no relief. I almost have to fall back on the cliché that time will heal and yet I know

that time will never heal completely, that Victoria will be with you always.

Please do accept my sad attempt at commiseration, though please also know that you and Lorraine are part of my thoughts and wishes for life that will inevitably go forward fruitfully.

Someone had considered Bill's loss as the father. It seems to have been the best support Bill got.

Four months after the stillbirth, seeking a change of scenery, the two of us went on a vacation. We stopped for a night at an historic Connecticut inn called Randall's Ordinary on our way up the East Coast to Maine, where we planned to meet Mark. It was the first vacation we had taken since Victoria's death, and it was difficult for me. I kept thinking it would have been our daughter's very first trip.

During breakfast at the inn, Bill and I were seated in a nearly empty part of the dining room beside a couple in their twenties with their one-year-old son. The boy gurgled and laughed and sucked on his eggs as his adoring parents cooed at him. Within fifteen minutes tears were rolling down my face. I grabbed my linen napkin, excused myself and stepped into the morning air. I stood outside the old building, built in the 1600s, and looked down a path into the woods. I imagined John Randall, the namesake of the inn, walking down that path to a long day's work. I thought of the women of his era and the children they lost.

A waitress, dressed in the historic garb of the day, opened the heavy, wooden door. Still teary, I turned to her. "I'm guessing breakfast can't be that bad," she said.

"No," I said. "I lost a baby in June and that baby in there, well, I just need a minute."

"I understand," she said. "I'm so sorry."

John Randall's old creaky gray door closed again. I dried my tears and went back inside. As I took my seat, I looked at the boy and smiled. His parents were none the wiser for my leaving or the deep grief that stirred whenever I saw little ones with their parents. After the family left, Bill and I sat alone, sipping our coffee, mostly quiet.

After a long silence, Bill offered, "It's going to happen."

"All the time," I replied.

As we got up and headed toward the door, the same waitress came bounding out of the kitchen. "Ma'am," she called out. I turned and she held before her a bouquet of flowers, emblazoned with fiery red, mustard yellow, royal velvet purple, and strong pink. The waitress had wrapped the stems in a wet paper towel and aluminum foil to keep them fresh. "God bless, ma'am," she said as she handed me the bouquet, then quickly looked down and returned to the kitchen. Instantly I smiled.

When I got back to our room, I put the flowers in a plastic water bottle. They stayed directly in front of me, held tight in a coffee cup holder, as we drove up the coast to Bar Harbor, and later when we returned home to New Jersey. *I will remember this bouquet to the day I die,* I told myself. Once again my spirit soared, having been touched by extraordinary kindness.

So many of these light-filled moments presented themselves that a peace started to well up in me. These gestures were not only for me but for my baby girl. *Victoria had touched all these lives, made all these moments possible.* I was calmed by that thought—calmed into recovery.

But what did it mean to recover, anyway? I wondered. *How will I know when I arrive?* While still on vacation in Maine, I talked with Mark about how I felt. He gazed out the window of the restaurant to the bay while I spoke, but said little. After Bill and I returned home and Mark to Chicago, he wrote me this email:

> *Recovering from a battle like the one you have just gone through will be slow. What did you expect? It will come to you, though not as quickly as you want it. Recovery doesn't mean forgetting, it means putting it all in perspective. I doubt you will ever get over some of the pain. This whole thing is one of those experiences that makes you who you are.*

I ruminated on that long and hard. *I won't get over it, I'll get used to it. I will emerge from recovery when I no longer feel like the old Lorraine. A new Lorraine will appear. I am already birthing her.*

If I had to pinpoint when I started the transformation, I would say it was just after Bill and I had learned Victoria had slipped away. It was when I heard my husband say to his mother on the phone, "We lost the baby." I was struck by how he had phrased that sentence. Never would I have thought to put it that way. He was right, of course. We had lost her, and yet we had not.

By the time I returned home from Maine, I began to glean that recovery meant accepting loss of the physical baby even as I began to recognize her spiritual presence was still with me. No person taught me this, but Mark's pastoral attention to my every thought and feeling encouraged me to follow what was first a tenuous instinct. For that kindness I will forever be grateful.

In my dazed and weepy state just out of the hospital I sat at my dining room table, day in and day out, reading books, writing poems, listening to the radio. In these simple ways insights and spiritual comforts came to me. Around the time of Victoria's delivery the song *I Will Remember You* by Sarah McLachlan hit the charts. The lyrics haunted me:

> *I will remember you*
> *Will you remember me?*
> *Don't let your life pass you by*
> *Weep not for the memories.*

Whenever I heard the song I would say to my daughter, *I'll always remember you, Victoria.*

The day the July 1999 edition of *Harper's* magazine arrived I read a story about a father who privately buried his infant son. I devoured the story. It was about someone like me. The writer, George Michelsen Foy, a novelist, described in such detail his frail son's unsuccessful attempt to grasp life. He remembered those few days, a lifetime for his son:

> ...when I was trying to help Olivier amid the no-time of ICU neon, I lived harder and more intensely than I ever had in my forty-four years of existence. I lived so intensely, and, in many ways, happily, that the only memory that even came close was the very first few days of falling in love, or a trip I had taken in the Hindu Kush mountains, during which my life was sometimes at risk.

That made me think of transcendent moments in my life: hearing my sixth-grade teacher proclaim a poem I wrote about an angel wonderful; walking into St. Peter's Basilica and hearing the choir singing; standing before a huge golden Buddha at a monastery in Japan; reading the last page of the novel A Prayer for Owen Meany; and seeing the gleam in Bill's eyes for the first time. On all those occasions life had burst into flames inside me and illumined some mystery.

Life, I have decided, is the sacred teacher. If God speaks, surely one of his languages is the unfolding of events. The day I realized this I let go of the middle-men—the priests, the gurus, the channelers, the seers, and all the so-called interpreters of reality—who consider themselves the dispensers of meaning. Ever since, life in all its detail has become my experience of God.

On that first vacation after Victoria died, Bill and I strolled along the beach at Cape Cod every day at sunset. One afternoon Bill went off to photograph seals and surfs. As I stood on the shore's edge I felt the wind in my hair, in my lungs, and on my skin as my mind unraveled. The sun sprinkled gold dust on the sand—an imaginary gold that glowed orange-yellow. The ocean reflected the sky's lavender light and the water's surface shimmered with a strange and heavenly patina.

That day the sunset taught me how it's possible for Victoria to be here and not be here. *Victoria is the gold, the lavender, the light, the beauty that is breathtaking but cannot be held or contained.*

Months later, I got to thinking that reality also includes personal interactions that take a different turn from what we expect—different from what we would have them take. These interactions, some of them very brief, are not all shaped by the standard social cookie cutter. I thought of the unlikely individuals who became some of my best life teachers, the ones who helped me discover what is inside me and showed me how to move on following tragedy.

As a cub reporter in my early twenties I developed a rapport with a police officer on my beat. One day when I was visiting the traffic division, where he worked, he told me he lived a couple of blocks away. "I would like you to meet my family," he said. Since he was on his lunch hour we walked to his home. Two small children played quietly on the floor in his modern comfortable living room, while his wife, a short, dark-haired woman with a ready smile, read a magazine at the island in the kitchen. We exchanged pleasantries and I thought, *What a great life this man has. A perfect family. Everything seems right...I'll have this someday.*

The officer and I walked back to the station when he said, "I have a beautiful family, don't I?"

"Yes," I said. "Thank you for introducing me."

"It's my replacement family," he said. I stopped walking, my brow furrowed. "You heard me. Five years ago I left for work. My wife put our two kids in the car to take them grocery shopping. The three-month-old was in his car seat. They never made it to the store. An eighteen-wheeler hit them and they were dead on impact. That driver wiped out my whole family in one second."

I did not know what to say. "I started over again," he went on. "I like you, kid, and I hope you never have to go through anything like that but, if you do, I want to tell you something. Don't wait until you're ready to get back into life because you know what? You're never going to be ready. Just get back in. Don't let anything pass you by."

What impelled him to share his story, and in such a way, I will never know. It was the only time he ever offered a glimpse into his personal life.

Another time I was sitting on a beat-up couch in an airplane hangar interviewing an aerobatics pilot on a hot August day. He had just been in the sky, his plane spinning and diving, but at that moment his assistant, having folded up the wings of the aircraft, was wheeling it inside. The pilot and I talked about G-force and training and national competitions when the conversation suddenly switched gears.

"What made you want to do this to begin with?" I asked.

He pointed to homes on the other side of the runway, where he had grown up gazing at the sky and watching in wonder as one particular championship pilot practiced his routines. One day he ventured into the very hangar in which we were sitting and approached that champ, who became his teacher and his father figure. The two of them flew together, the pilot recalled, and as he spoke I envisioned the older pilot's hand on that of a teenage boy, guiding it over the meters and lights and instruments in the cockpit. In my mind's eye I saw the boy looking back at the champion in awe. It turned out the champion died young in a motorcycle accident and his student, then a man, took over the hangar.

"You must miss flying together," I said.

The aerobatics star did not miss a beat. "But, m'am," he said. "We still do."

What names did I have for these encounters? Would I want to do without even one of them? No. My Victoria was the greatest of those teachers. I could think of her as my dead daughter, and our relationship would end, leaving at least a part of me for the rest of my life in a cold stasis. Or, based upon my faith and my experience of Victoria's continued presence, I could think of her as someone with whom I could keep sharing a spiritual relationship I could never before have fathomed.

There were planes on which Victoria and I could still fly together. I chose to accept her presence without further questioning. There was more joy in that decision and more warmth, too. That decision continues to bring me peace and allows me to deepen my relationship with my blessed daughter.

One day my cousin Kathy talked to me about Meaghan, her first daughter who had died of a heart malady after living only days. "There are times," she said, "when I feel—no, I *know*—that my daughter is with me. There are days when the sense of having Meaghan as an otherworldly guardian is as palpable as running my fingers through the grass."

Then Kathy, a scientist, told me a ghost story. Her bravery in sharing this story touched me. Five years after Meaghan's death, shortly after settling into a new home, Kathy awoke in the middle of the night. In the darkness she saw an apparition of a curly haired girl who looked under the bed, into the closet, and then vanished. The girl was about the age her daughter would have been. Kathy was sure it was Meaghan.

"One thought ran through my mind," Kathy said. "I thought, *My God, Meaghan's been with us all along. We had moved and she was checking out the new digs.*"

Did Kathy really see the ghost? I think she did, yet I don't know. But I will tell you this: In the middle of the night, I watch.

CHAPTER ELEVEN

Finding Peace

*D*uring the first couple of months after the still-birth, I noticed I looked at little girls in the store too intently. They sensed it. Their gazes lingered when they looked back. They offered me toys. Sometimes they smiled at me as if they knew I was Victoria's mother.

As summer passed into fall, I realized I usually had no problem being in the presence of children with their innocent stares and chubby hands and plastic bags of Cheerios. My enthusiasm for them flowed freely, as it used to do, except when I came upon a girl who could be Victoria. If I met a Chinese girl or an African American girl I could stay clear-minded and happy and play with her. But if she was fair-skinned and light-haired, as my Victoria would have been, I got a knot in my throat. I got lost in an emotion without a name as if it were a dense, dark forest.

If it had not been for people's words of love pushing me forward, I would have stayed locked in the longing for my little girl forever, while contemplating someone else's little girl, mesmerized by her. Years earlier I read an account of a Nazi concentration camp survivor who kept his sanity through his horrendous ordeal by closing his eyes and contemplating the image of his wife. In his mind he would behold his beloved and that was enough. I understood this survival technique. Merely conjuring the image of Victoria in my arms was enough to calm me—enough to have made my lifetime worthwhile.

Victoria's image made me peaceful, but it also made me sad. Most certainly it did not make me the kind of mother I still wanted to be. I wanted to nag somebody about wearing a sweater in questionably cool weather and about eating right and going to bed on time. I told myself, *I will try again to have a baby.* The determination to do that rose like a phoenix from the ashes right after Victoria's baptism. At a time when I was still dazed by life's sudden and cruel blow, it astonished me that this spark of desire welled up from my pain and despair. It was tantamount to someone being thrown from a horse, breaking both legs, being in traction, and saying, "I can't wait to ride again." The feeling was illogical and ridiculous. Yet there was the desire. I could deny or wrestle with it, but it was there.

I knew I would try again. I had gotten pregnant with Victoria at the age of thirty-nine on the first try, which seemed miraculous. But I also knew a repeat of that happy fate was most unlikely. I was forty and did not have forever to try. Frankly, I just might not succeed.

Then what? What would I do with these impulses of mine, this desire to be a mother that shot itself off like a flare inside me during my darkest hours?

Then came Nicholas, a charmer of a boy. Bill and I met him on a chance encounter at a Friendly's restaurant. We had no sooner slid into our booths and ordered turkey dinners when I saw two little eyes peek at me from the booth next to us. My husband turned to see what entranced me so. We were both watching intently when two-year-old Nicholas stood up in his seat and looked at each of us before breaking into a grin and clapping his hands in front of him. He showed us the picture of trucks he had crayoned and pointed out they were carrying logs on top. Then he touched my husband's nose and giggled. He was a burst of ebullience.

I observed him closely. His eyes were not quite slanted, his hair not quite black and I thought he might be Asian. Nicholas was out for a meal with his father, a big friendly Caucasian man, older than Bill and I, and his father's buddy. The father, who owned a logging company, introduced himself and quickly engaged us in conversation. He told us that he and his wife had adopted their son from Kazakhstan, a country located on the northwest corner of China just west of Mongolia. Formerly Kazakhstan was part of the Soviet Union. The father explained how it had been only three months from the time he and his wife decided to adopt to actually holding Nicholas, then ten weeks old, in their arms. "There was such a shortage of milk that the hospital was happy to let

Nicholas go," the new father said. "The children were on rations. Ten babies shared the equivalent of one bottle." He and his wife bonded with Nicholas instantly, and he to them. They named him after the czar of Russia. The adoption went so well the couple adopted another baby from the same orphanage, a girl they named Kara for the city in which both she and Nicholas had been born, Karaganda.

I could not take my gaze off Nicholas, who stole my heart for good when he finally picked up his picture and tried to put it in his father's pocket. "Home," he said. "Show mama. Show mama." There was something about how his lips pursed when he uttered the words, something about how urgently important it was to him to show his artwork to his mother, that unexpectedly put me at peace with the idea of adoption. Nicholas and his picture of trucks and logs brought me to an understanding that there are many paths to motherhood and that each of them was as real as any other.

I had known people, too many to count, who disliked, even hated, their biological mothers. I had known women who cried at the suggestion they may grow to be like their mothers, and mothers who had given birth to children whom they would as soon disown. There was in these cases biology but no love. Here was Nicholas, the embodiment of the opposite. I now thought, *There are a lot of places to put my maternal instincts to good use and many lives that need to be touched, many hearts that need to be filled.*

Just as the meaning of motherhood began to expand inside me, other words also took on different meanings. Take "loss." I smiled at the thought of how difficult it used to be for me to clean out my office or the attic or a closet. *No, I could not possibly do without that hat or without five jackets,* I convinced myself. It used to be I would not dream of throwing away a book. I did not want to lose anything. The loss of a thing meant the loss of my emotional attachment to that thing and all it symbolized, whether it was a time of youth, the memory of a place, or the potential of something that long ago had fallen fallow.

After Victoria, that all changed. To lose a life my body and spirit had been feeding and nurturing for nine months felt like the pinnacle of helplessness. Before Victoria died I was a controller of agendas and schedules and the business of life. I had exercised every modicum of control I could muster, and then some, to ensure Victoria's safe arrival in the world, and I lost her anyway despite all my best efforts. I ruminated, *Could there be a better way for the universal order of things to show me my own insignificance? To show me the futility of control?*

Once a heartbeat is lost, there is nothing more precious that can be lost. Once I felt a life die within me, once I lost the very thing I would have given over all my earthly belongings to save, everything else seemed so very small. The need to keep things and to clutch them close to my bosom fell away. After Victoria, I could clean out an attic in no time. After all, my very soul had been cleaned out.

After my baby died I started seeing the world as if it were an x-ray. I saw to the core of people and situations. I could easily see past the surfaces to the guts. The guts of everything and everyone was a life force, valued for its potency, beneficence, potential for warmth. This kind of vision made a difference in relationships, in living, in writing, in loving. I realized the urge to keep only those things that are essential rests on the assumption that the owner of the things can see what is essential about them.

The lesson of seeing what is essential in life was punctuated three-and-a-half months after Victoria's death. My family had been following the trail of Hurricane Floyd as it blew up the East Coast. It was a tropical storm when it touched down on North Jersey but it still had a lot of power to vent, with a vengeance.

The day after the hurricane, family members and friends trudged through my parents' flooded house, which usually sat prettily along the calm, rolling Saddle River. We started the arduous cleanup after the river's mighty waters contaminated with sewage had ravaged their home. The muddy water had destroyed Dad's law and personal libraries, two floors' worth of carpeting, two cars, and numerous other household items. It was difficult to see their meticulous home turned into a mud-covered mess. It was in the sorting and throwing out of things that the tragedy behind the tragedy became unveiled.

All of us had formed a human chain, sending the books from hand to hand up from the basement to the

first floor where they were sorted. Salvageable ones
went into a wheelbarrow and out to the front lawn
where we spread them on bed sheets to dry in the sun.
Dozens of black garbage bags filled with books made
their way through the chain and onto a mountainous
heap at the curb. What a heartbreak. Those soggy bags
contained the history of my father's law career, including books lovingly supplemented and opened and read
for decades. Those bags also contained a major part of
my upbringing. Dad always referred to his books in our
many conversations during my youth—the three-volume
set on Churchill, the four-volume set on Lincoln,
numerous books by great philosophers.

Hours rolled by, and the front yard slowly filled with
volumes. The process was interrupted only when my
father every so often said, "I was hoping to die with this
still on my desk." Treasured books shared space on the
lawn with debris that had flowed downstream, including
a vat of soy sauce from the Chinese restaurant half a mile
away, a kid's basketball set, part of a porch, bagged
garbage, clothes, and a ladder.

A book of poetry by Rudyard Kipling and a tub of somebody's driveway sealant were all the same to the Saddle
River and Hurricane Floyd. The river picked up and
destroyed possessions, even whole houses, and knocked
out phone lines. Thousands lived with the dirt and musty
stench for weeks. *The river even stole lives, for no good
reason, just like Victoria's was stolen,* I thought as I surveyed
the damage and loss. It was as if I was witnessing a physi-

cal manifestation of my emotional damage and loss, just three months out from Victoria's death.

The truth was as clear as it was going to get for me. My truth was this: *We are a part of nature and sooner or later we must yield as its victims.* The great flood was a reminder of how little power people have. In the biggest battles between nature and humanity, nature wins.

Another word that took on new meaning for me after Victoria's death was "perfection." In my twenties, I pursued perfection intrepidly only to discover somewhere in my thirties that the pursuit was fruitless because perfection could not be defined, much less attained. One person's perfection was another's sorrow and yet another's irrelevance. Yet I would still strike out and try to achieve it sometimes.

At forty and without my daughter, I relinquished the pursuit of perfection for good. After the stillbirth I felt like a miner returning empty-handed from a gold rush. All that effort, all that promise, all that hope for naught.

Perfection is about controlling all aspects of some ideal, some project. Even if perfection were possible, by the nature of things, it would only last a moment before changing. Everything changes all the time. I had lost control of the ultimate goal, and, when I did, I abandoned the illusion of control in all other things, which were, by definition, lesser. I expected that would feel limiting, awful. I was amazed to discover as early as six months after the stillbirth my surrender to imperfection made me feel free. After the shock and the agony, after the tears and the lamenting, after the railing of the unanswerable "why" into the cosmos, there was strange freedom. The eerie, chilling silence of the stillbirth had given way to the warm, comforting silence of peace.

Above all, I had made peace with Victoria. I felt this peace when I entered the nursery, which in the earliest days after Victoria's death filled me with so much sorrow that to set foot in it would make me cry. Yet I did not want to take apart the nursery because it was Victoria's spot. It was a memorial to Victoria, her place in this world, and to dismantle it would erase the last vestige of her presence in our home.

After I had made some peace my friend Karen walked into Victoria's room for the first time. A dread hung over her like stalactites in a cave. For a few minutes she stood quietly, resting her hand on the empty crib, then she reached down to squeeze My Pal Al, a green stuffed toy that would have been one of Victoria's firsts. She looked at *The Original Mother Goose*, an oversized purple book, which was to have been my baby's first storybook. "It's peaceful here," she said. "I don't know what I expected, but I like it."

I did, too. Some days I went into the nursery, sat in the rocker, looked over at the urn and talked to Victoria's spirit. "I am still your mother, Victoria. Let me know if you need anything; I will do my best to help." Those times were important. I did not want to become passive in our ongoing relationship. I knew there was more that Victoria, in her state, could do for me than I could do for her, but I liked to offer my help. Maybe what she needed was for me to ask her if she needed anything. Maybe she was waiting for me to ask.

So where is Victoria now? What is she? An angel? When an angel shows up in Biblical accounts, it generally is not to reveal a truth but rather to announce a beginning, usually a birth. It is almost always like that—angels and births go together. Perhaps my Victoria always was an angel. Some people tell me she may have come to me so I could learn lessons. Maybe, but I am uncomfortable with how egocentric that seems.

Certainly Victoria has stretched my capacity to love far beyond what it used to be. "As the Father has loved me, so have I loved you; abide in my love." Some days I feel these words were spoken not only by Jesus to his followers but by Victoria to me. I live with those words because I live with that part of her that has endured—her love. I do not know if Victoria is an angel. I know only she is an angel to me.

In one of the dozens of condolence cards and letters I received, this was written: "You have a wonderful eternal relationship to look forward to in that place where God Himself will wipe away all tears and there will be no more sorrow. King David shared that hope so eloquently in Scripture—'I shall go to him'—when his small son went to glory."

"Went to glory." I liked that. Who would have thought life would put me in the same situation as King

David? The condolence note led me to reread 2 Samuel 12:22-23:

> He said, "While the child was still alive, I fasted and wept; for I said, 'Who knows whether the Lord will be gracious to me, that the child may live?' But now he is dead; why should I fast? Can I bring him back again? I shall go to him, but he will not return to me."

Victoria has changed the face of death for me, just as the death of David's child changed it for him. I still do not want death, but I do not dread it, and that is a very large gift of peace. When pregnant I looked forward to the day when I would take walks with Victoria, her delicate hand in mine. I imagined squeezing her hand and looking at her lovingly as she studied her shoes, or pointed at a bee, or squinted in the sun. One day, we will have our walk.

I have a vision of my own death. I am walking into the light, being led by my daughter, forever a girl, her little hand in mine. "Hey, Piccolina," I will say. "It's Mommy." She will know and we will walk into eternity. Together.

CHAPTER TWELVE

❀

A Virtual Memorial

*T*hree months after the stillbirth, Bill and I felt the need to do something in Victoria's honor and to share the beginnings of our newfound serenity with loved ones. The baptism in the hospital had been a small, private ceremony, and we had not wanted any other larger, more public event. Another service would have felt like ripping open a wound that had just begun to heal. We were searching for a special way to honor our daughter's life and remember her in death. That is when Bill came up with the marvelous idea of a "virtual service." It took months for me to write it, and then months for him to read and add to it. In the end, it took longer to birth the service than it did to grow the baby, but that was okay. Such endeavors create their own timetables.

Each person who received the "service" in the mail opened a large envelope on which was printed this invitation:

Bill and Lorraine Ash
loving parents of

VICTORIA HELEN ASH

stillborn one year ago on June 2, 1999

invite our family and friends to join us
in honoring her soul and celebrating her little life
by taking quiet time to contemplate the enclosed memorial

Inside the envelope was an excerpt from this book, a donation card for the perinatal support program in the hospital where Victoria was delivered, and a sheet entitled "Highlights of a Life." That sheet featured a drawing of Victoria created by Bill and concluded with this description:

She was 21 inches long, weighed 6 pounds 13 ounces, and had the prettiest hands and pink face. We'll never know the color of her eyes. They opened in heaven.

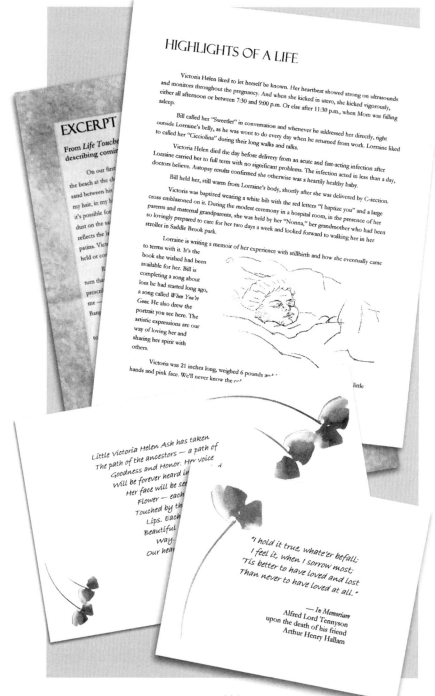

HIGHLIGHTS OF A LIFE

Victoria Helen liked to let herself be known. Her heartbeat showed strong on ultrasounds and monitors throughout the pregnancy. And when she kicked in utero, she kicked vigorously, either all afternoon or between 7:30 and 9:00 p.m. Or else after 11:30 p.m., when Mom was falling asleep.

Bill called her "Sweetlet" in conversation and whenever he addressed her directly, right outside Lorraine's belly, as he was wont to do every day when he returned from work. Lorraine liked to called her "Cicciolina" during their long walks and talks.

Victoria Helen died the day before delivery from an acute and fast-acting infection after Lorraine carried her to full term with no significant problems. The infection acted in less than a day, doctors believe. Autopsy results confirmed she otherwise was a heartily healthy baby. Bill held her, still warm from Lorraine's body, shortly after she was delivered by C-section.

Victoria was baptized wearing a white bib with the red letters "I baptize you" and a large cross emblazoned on it. During the modest ceremony in a hospital room, in the presence of her parents and maternal grandparents, she was held by her "Nonna," her grandmother who had been so lovingly prepared to care for her two days a week and looked forward to walking her in her stroller in Saddle Brook park.

Lorraine is writing a memoir of her experience with stillbirth and how she eventually came to terms with it. It's the book she wished had been available for her. Bill is completing a song about loss he had started long ago, a song called *When You're Gone*. He also drew the portrait you see here. The artistic expressions are our way of loving her and sharing her spirit with others.

Victoria was 21 inches long, weighed 6 pounds a⌷ hands and pink face. We'll never know the co⌷

little

Little Victoria Helen Ash has taken
The path of the ancestors — a path of
Goodness and Honor. Her voice
Will be forever heard in⌷
Her face will be se⌷
Flower — each⌷
Touched by th⌷
Lips. Each⌷
Beautiful⌷
way-⌷
Our hea⌷

---

*"I hold it true, whate'er befall;
I feel it, when I sorrow most;
'Tis better to have loved and lost
Than never to have loved at all."*

— *In Memoriam*
Alfred Lord Tennyson
upon the death of his friend
Arthur Henry Hallam

There were also two poetic tributes to Victoria from Cherokee friends.

HUMBLE THOUGHTS FOR BABY VICTORIA

Little Victoria Helen Ash has taken
The path of the ancestors—a path of
Goodness and Honor. Her voice
Will be forever heard in the wind.
Her face will be seen in every
Flower—each rose will be
Touched by the moisture of her
Lips. Each day will be more
Beautiful because she passed our
Way. When sadness touches
Our hearts she will smile and whisper,
I am only a breath away.

—Marti MomFeather

TO OUR LITTLE SISTER

May our Mother the Earth guide your tiny feet,
May our Father the Sky keep his arms around you,
May our Grandmother the Sun warm your cold days,
May our Grandfather the Moon
keep the light in your heart,
May the Star People light their fires
on your path to Heaven,
and may the Holy Spirit always shield you
from the pain.
Blessings to you, Victoria Helen Ash.

—Brian Standing Bear

Many people who received the virtual service said it gave them a window into the experience, a way to see what was happening inside Bill and me even if they could not feel exactly how we felt.

Reading their responses sent more waves of calm over me and helped me reach an even deeper inner peace with the fate Victoria and I shared. For her sake, for mine, and for the sake of a child who may yet come. Every child deserves a mother's whole attention. I knew it would be sad when the day came to take Victoria's urn out of the nursery and put it somewhere else, maybe on a shelf in my home office, to make way for another child. But I also knew Victoria would understand. She would remain my constant companion, more accepting than the closest friend.

She would remain sugar and spice and everything nice. What I remember most blessedly about pregnancy was the feeling I was never alone. Now I know I will have that feeling all my life.

CHAPTER THIRTEEN

❀

Getting Through the Holidays

I was leery of Halloween. It had been only five months since I delivered Victoria. Vividly I recalled handing out chocolate bars to trick-or-treaters the year before. My belly was just starting to swell and I had anticipated walking Victoria around in her stroller through our neighborhood on her first Halloween. I had imagined Victoria somehow would absorb the fun of it all even though she would have been a newborn. Bill suggested we could dress her up in an orange outfit and pretend she was a pumpkin. But all that was not to be.

Halloween night I stood at the door alone, ready to toss candies into hundreds of plastic pumpkins, and cotton bags lovingly sewn by mothers to match the costumes of their little darlings. "There are so many children this year," my neighbor told me across our lawns. I smiled politely, yet thought, *One is missing.*

The first child arrived—a little girl by herself. Her protective father, hands in his jeans' pockets, waited on the sidewalk as she came up the walkway. I expected my breath to catch, to choke, and to have to push my resentment down my throat as I handed out those candies. But I also had grown used to not knowing what to expect from myself from hour to hour. Before Victoria, I was very much a stiff upper lip kind of person. I fortified myself against the world and let things bounce off me, not seep into me. Since Victoria's arrival, everything seeps in and comes out. I cry a lot easier and laugh more heartily.

Instinctively, I did something I had never before done. The girl walked toward my front door, basket swinging on her arm. She wore a pastel blue jumper over a white silky blouse. Her black hair was bobbed at her chin. Her eyes, glittered in blue, opened wide as she approached. In that quiet, enchanted way girls have, she said, "Trick or treat." I went down on one knee and looked at her, really looked at her. "I'm from *The Wizard of Oz*," she said. Her face broke into a shy smile. I tossed a foil-wrapped white chocolate ghost and a miniature Snickers bar into her basket as I admired her costume. "Dorothy, you sure look pretty." She backed away, still smiling. "Thank you," she said, before spinning around and looking at her father in the street. She faced me again and breathed a sigh of contentment. "Happy Halloween," she said.

As she walked away, she turned back one last time, so quickly her hair caught in the the low-lying dogwood tree in my yard. "Happy Halloween," she repeated as she lifted her arms to free her hair. In the happiness of her eyes I fancied I could see the woman she would become.

Later, Marilyn Monroe came by in a white slinky dress, her face shiny, her lips ruby. "Trick or treat," she said. I knelt to greet Marilyn, and dozens of other children who followed throughout the evening. For hours I had a great time, enjoying all the children more than I ever had before. I even enjoyed the little boy who politely declined all ten kinds of candy I had offered him. "Sorry," he said, earnestly. "I just don't like any of them. But thanks anyway."

Darkness began to fall when a group of five children came by. This time, my husband stood at the door with a bowl of goodies. "Everybody, stop!" one little guy called out. "Everybody, stop. I dropped some candy." The masqueraders halted on our lawn and searched for the lost sweets. Bill and I laughed.

Odd, isn't it, that a dead child could open me to this wondrous world as much as a live one? I had seen it, delighted, from the outside before, but my view was from the height of adulthood, not at eye level with the little people. On that Halloween I knew that grieving Victoria had transmuted into a new way for me to be in the world. My knowing things through feeling them, my hair-trigger emotion was part of the legacy of Victoria's brief life.

In situation after situation I found myself seeing with new eyes. My heart jerked before my brain engaged. I was riding my emotions like a raft in white water. It dawned on me, *So this is who I am.* That controlled and unemotional person I used to be had vanished.

The world of children opened up to me again and again. Just as I saw in children traces of the adults they would become, I saw in adults glimmers of the children they had been—and not in the heady way of Freudian theory or in the intellectual language of the many socio-logical and psychological studies I had read in college. This was different. Continuity clicked. Life, I could say, began anew.

In the wreckage left by the flood that destroyed so much in my parents' home was a chest that was headed for the garbage heap. My brother axed it open to find treas-ured photographs from our childhood. He and my sister-in-law dried them, and one day we spent a couple of hours looking over them. "Look at Mom. Look at Dad," I marveled. "Look how young they are. Ted, look at us. Just look at us." I was moved to tears by one faded and damaged photo of my mother, so young, sitting at her kitchen table and feeding me by bottle. I understood the photograph. I had those photos restored, had negatives and reprints made, and organized them into multiple col-lages for framing to give my family members for Christmas. The images were reminders of our collective growth and love and I wanted them around me. I was tuned into myself as a child, into all children.

In the fall of 1999 I discovered, as if by magic, a letter from Childreach, a worldwide humanitarian organization that links sponsors to more than one million needy children in forty impoverished countries. This was the first time I had opened a letter from Childreach. For years I had tossed away countless envelopes from the group. For 66 cents a day, the letter said, I could give life-saving support to a child. "The difference between despair and hope costs pennies a day," the pitch went on. I could write to "my" child, too, and my child could write to me. We could even visit. I signed up, choosing to sponsor a girl of any age from any country. In this way ten-year-old Annie Rose of the Philippines came into my life. This was how our caring for each other began. Why did I open the letter then? Why did I get involved? Victoria.

I also wrote a letter to the American Indian Relief Council to which I had contributed for years. It was really only a jotted note. "Here I sit among the affluent," I wrote. "There you sit amid poverty. Doesn't it seem there should be something more I can do?"

One afternoon the phone rang. A woman from the relief council introduced herself. "I had to call back personally," she said. "I just read your note." People on the Rosebud and Pine Ridge reservations in South Dakota needed a lot of life's necessities. The elders prized blankets and heavy thick socks, she said, and children desperately needed clothing, toys, disposable diapers. "We have people who are washing disposables and re-using them," the woman said. "That's the kind of need I'm talking about."

I thought of Victoria's wardrobe, toys in her crib, and the bags of disposable diapers that sat in her dresser, unused. I thought how pleased she would be to have other little girls wearing her clothes and playing with her toys.

Although in the end I could not part with my baby's things, I did write a check and send it to Rapid City so that necessities would materialize for the children there.

Meanwhile, Victoria's things were necessities for me at home. The pink dresses hanging in the nursery closet and undershirts in her dresser were the few visible signs that Victoria was a part of our lives. The presence of her things also kept alive the dream of another child perhaps arriving someday. Making room for the things in my house was making room for new possibility in my life.

Fate put me in yet another situation concerning the welfare of a child in the months after my daughter's delivery. I found myself on a jury deliberating a sexual assault case involving a nine-year-old girl and a grown man who was a friend of her family. *I will listen to the facts and assess them*, I thought, and that is exactly what I did.

During the trial, I sat listening to the testimony of the girl's father. He said he told his daughter always to call out for him if she was in trouble. He told her that as long as daddy was around nothing would harm her. His voice broke and he held his head in his hands as he added, "I let this happen in my own house." Tears streamed down my cheeks and I made no effort to stop myself. I could not believe I was crying in public. My tears continued to flow when the little girl described what had happened to her.

I thought I was totally settled with the notion I had had a daughter who had not lived. In November I had even read a part of this book, when it was still a growing manuscript, at my hospital during its First Annual Walk to Remember. This service was in memory of babies who had died by miscarriage, ectopic pregnancy or stillbirth, and those who had lived a very short time.

Overall, I was accepting of Victoria's stillbirth—except for the darkness in a corner of my heart during the holiday season. Something special seemed to be happening in the life of everyone around me. Reminders of Victoria were everywhere, even when I watched a documentary on Jackie Kennedy Onassis, a woman who really knew loss. The show presented her whole life—her work, her children, her loves, and her losses. She had lost a baby through stillbirth and another through miscarriage and another as an infant. Then she had lost a husband. She gave sadness an elegant, dignified face but, even when well-dressed, it was sadness all the same.

I watched the Christmas festivities as if they were a movie being played inside a bright crystal ornament. By the first week of December, Victoria had been dead six months. All around me there were lights and Santas and parents busily preparing to make the season magical for their children. I had just enough buoyancy to reenter life, enough innate optimism to smile and feel some of the happiness around me. It was the first year I can remember that Christmas shopping was not a hassle; it was easy. I had special ideas for everyone I knew who had helped me through Victoria's death, and I simply bought them presents, not worrying about the cost.

Mark got a diamond stud earring, my mother a faceted crystal jewelry box, and Bill a tuxedo. *Certainly there is enough in life to be thankful for,* I told myself. Still there was a part of me where the lights most definitely were out. I did not articulate much during those months. It seemed talking about Victoria would disturb the festivities around me. In the season of the baby Jesus and his miraculous birth, it seemed odd to be talking of the miracles of change wrought by a baby's death.

I was out of sync with almost everyone and tried to shield many of my friends from the full, ongoing intensity of my grief. Occasionally I got teary-eyed at the sight of a little girl or whenever something around me triggered a memory. To stop and explain all these delicate moments, their origins and the places of pain to which they took my emotions, was too tiring. Sometimes I did articulate just what I was feeling and thinking but the effort usually was met with stares of disapproval or blankness. Many people, I figured out, saw my processing what I felt as wallowing. They were wrong, but I needed my energy to heal myself, not enlighten them. Consequently, I kept a lot inside me.

Once when I expressed my grief, a friend responded, "The pain you feel has been going on for thousands of years, for as long as there have been humans, and there is nothing distinctive or special about it." When viewed in the big picture, he noted, it just did not amount to much. I thought, *Isn't enlightenment supposed to come with compassion?*

After that, I left even more unsaid and got to feeling very alone. Another friend suggested it might help if I let myself cry. Inherent in the statement was a world of misunderstanding. *How could I not cry? Had she not noticed the fundamental shifts in me?* I imagined my personal transformation was as obvious as the aftermath of an earthquake. The notion of giving myself permission to cry was akin to suggesting to the sky that it let itself rain. Crying was a reflex. No permission needed. My friend did not understand that. She could not and I understood she could not. Still, that did not satiate my need to be understood.

In addition to my husband and my cousin Kathy, both of whom were survivors of the same or similar tragedy, I could fling open the doors to my strange mental landscape to only one person, Mark. He knew despair and weakness because of his own life battles following the deaths of his parents and his divorce, and he was beginning to understand how to pull strength from those experiences. He knew me, too, through many seasons of my life. We could share and hold each other's pain. To me it was important to talk with a person who had not lived my fate. To be able to speak freely with someone in the great river of life gave me hope that I someday could rejoin it fully. For the time being, I felt like I was in a tributary. Off to the side. Not out of the water but not in the main currents either.

Perhaps I chose Mark because he was willing to sit with me in emotionally dark places; he was not a friend who brought light to me but rather one who spent time in my darkness and then accompanied me as I found my own light. Maybe it was because he cried so very much when Victoria died and afterward, and let me see his grief. Perhaps it was because even long after the trauma, Mark coaxed me to open up to him again and again. He never tired of my grief, maybe because pain does not scare him or because he sees life head-on, as it is.

I knew I needed a realist; there were so many people ready to put a rose-colored window between me and reality. Some were downright ebullient when they heard about Victoria's stillbirth. "How wonderful!" one woman said with great sincerity. "You've given her eternal life. That must feel great." *Great?* I thought. *Are you crazy? Would you feel great if one of your daughters died? Why should I?*

Maybe I turned to Mark because he unabashedly acknowledged meaninglessness and that felt right, and because he simultaneously acknowledged any glimmer of good and that felt right, too. Maybe it was because he was honest enough to tell me I had to stop "copping an attitude" of superiority and anger whenever I encountered a mother I thought was neglectful of her child. For whatever reason, I let him join me as I roamed the full range of my varied states of mind.

I linked those shifting sands of consciousness to how I felt in the hospital when the fever was raging and I was freezing and shaking under two blankets. Before I fell asleep those nights I would go into a sort of twilight of the mind in which I pictured the things I still wanted to do in my life, the places I wanted to go, the people I wanted to spend time with, the things I could write. If only I did not succumb to the infection, if only I got more time.

Those nights I longed for the simple things I had taken for granted—every apple I had ever tasted, every hand I had ever held, every time I had breathed in sharp mountain air, every sip of coffee I had ever savored. I thought of those times at my computer writing late into the night, delighted when words met meaning and the two danced till dawn. *Oh, please, God, just one more night, just two more nights,* I thought. I had always loved those moments but while fighting for my life in that bed I recognized them for what they really are—gifts, possibilities in a world that owes me nothing.

Every day I thank God the fever passed and I rid myself of medications, but those panoramic shifts of consciousness remained. I was suspended in time and place on an ethereal plane where Victoria perhaps had gone. Even when tending to mundane tasks I seemed on the verge of new appreciations, new epiphanies.

One night I wrote to Mark about making a new chowder for dinner. As I stirred the ingredients with a wooden spoon the motion gave rise to the thought that the point of life is union. People with people, people with God, people with nature. Old school chums reminisce, a couple embraces, a painter chooses a landscape to portray—all their ecstasies are not inside them but in the union between them.

Ideas and emotions emerged from the mist, I wrote to Mark. In one missive, I described my vision of a woman walking into a village from the English moors at night. "I see her silhouette," I wrote. "She is veiled and I know she is coming into the village of my conscious mind. But I cannot see her face underneath the veil. I cannot see her eyes. She does not speak yet. She is still not here, but she is coming. Once we talk, she and I, I will pick up my pen and begin." Months later I realized that "woman" became *Life Touches Life*.

These states comforted, unsettled, and inspired me at the same time. I channeled everything I felt through Mark—the whole kaleidoscope, the emptiness, the rage, the gray feeling, while all about me were singing their songs of Noel. Mark even helped me to see that the states of mind I slipped into were a kind of superexcellent consciousness in which insight, emotion, and spirit converged. *Hasn't this been the kind of consciousness I have aspired to my whole life?* I wondered. Certainly. *Isn't this the achievement of years of striving?* Maybe. Either way, though, there it was at my feet—a holiday gift bundled in the most intense pain. In time I came to think of my strange states midway between here and heaven as a legacy of my daughter.

Someone else helped me through the holiday season, too—Annie Rose. Even though Victoria had died, I felt the urge to buy my daughter Christmas presents as if she could somehow receive them. But she could not receive the kind of present I would buy at a boutique or a toy shop. I could not buy that kind of present for my Victoria. But I could for

Annie Rose. She was not a niece or nephew who belonged with the other adults in my world. Annie and I were a globe apart but she belonged in my heart. We could reach across the world and touch one another with letters and encouragement and things. There were only miles between us and miles can be bridged. Victoria and I could not cross our vast divide in the same way.

When Childreach sent a periodic writeup, I loved to read about Annie. I received two pictures of her—one a portrait of her clad in a light pink T-shirt, shoulder-length hair shiny and black, expression serious, eyes a hundred years old. In the other she was with her father, a slight man in white pants and aqua-colored shirt. Father and daughter wore blue flip-flops and stood with austere expressions, side by side, in front of their home in a resettlement project some thirty-five miles from Manila. Her father was a factory worker, her mother made doormats from home and taught the neighbors about recycling. In the family there were five other children. As the oldest, Annie had responsibility for taking care of them, preparing meals and helping with the wash. She went to school every day. My first donation probably bought her schoolbooks.

What a simple thing, but I found joy in it and even more happiness in buying just the perfect Christmas gift for Annie—a red shirt with a small heart made of red stones on the front. As I packaged it for sending I could not help wondering, *How many foster parents across the world do what they do in honor of some little one who is not with them in the flesh?*

CHAPTER FOURTEEN

❧

Let the Healing Begin

Within months of the stillbirth I began to see life as a string of opportunities to care. A kind word could be dropped into a casual conversation. The devastation of a flood could be eased by offering help and reassurance. A request to help a child on the other side of the world could be answered. Opportunities are always present.

When people first started telling me how much they admired my strength in coping with Victoria's death, I told them my strength came from them. After a while, I got even clearer: My strength came from a realigned vision of life, people, and God. The emotional and physical chaos of Victoria's death had done violence to my heart, mind, and body. My physiology, spirituality, psychology—my whole life—had changed. If there is a good side to violence, it is in jumbling up all the pieces so they can be rearranged. In my new perspective, every small kindness shown me was a big deal because it helped me reconnect with others, with life and with myself.

In fall 1999 I spent a weekend at a writing retreat in the Catskills with six writers I had come to know. We convened there a couple of times a year. After a day of writing critiques, my teacher, Pat, and I walked from the retreat house across a quiet country road to the writers' cottages. Pat, the mother of four, is some twenty-five years older than I am. I think of her as my literary mother, someone who nurtures me as a writer and knows me intimately. As we walked side by side, enveloped by the soft darkness of a country night, she uttered two words, smiling. "You're up." I thought, *I am up. I am standing. The still-birth happened five months ago and I am out in the world doing my thing.* For the first time since Victoria's death I felt proud of myself. "Up" carries lots of meanings. Up and walking. Up in spirit. Up toward the heavens. Prize fighters get up. *I am up.*

When we reached our two cottages, nestled in the woods, we stood between them. Lanterns cast just enough light to illuminate the steps and front door to each. Before Pat and I departed, she extended one hand and gently pulled my head toward hers. She kissed me on the forehead and when she let go, I saw the light glisten in her wet eyes. Since then I have carried that kindness with me and I have become more aware of what I say. *Even one short sentence holds such power,* I remind myself, almost daily. *One short sentence can spark another's rebirth.*

Victoria helped me understand good words and deeds are the main agenda of life rather than niceties reserved for when there are resources to spare. For the first time I knew

I was alive in order to be kind. I also realized how much of my strength ultimately came from the kindnesses of others.

In August, three months after the stillbirth, I needed an endoscopy to diagnose whether there was an ulcer in my stomach following a bout of gastritis, a post-pregnancy complication. Even though this test required a tube down my throat and into my stomach, it did not add up to much after the physical trials I endured with the stillbirth and my life-threatening fever afterwards. Yet, I was not looking forward to one more medical procedure.

The night before the endoscopy I received an email from Mark sending good wishes for my procedure the next day. "I love you so much," he wrote, once again reaching out to offer comfort and compassion when I needed it. Another email arrived from my friend, Karen, "I'll hold good thoughts for you tomorrow."

The next morning with my husband at my side, holding my hand, a nurse linked me to an intravenous tube and wheeled my gurney into the endoscopy suite. A technician placed a plastic cup in my mouth, and began to slide the thin tube through the cup, down my throat, and into my gut. As the anesthesia flowed into my brain, I felt like a leaf on a breeze. Kind words drifted over the landscape of my mind, which was then an uneasy, frightening place—*I love you.*" "*I'll hold good thoughts.*" This became the first of many times when I began to accept and receive love from others in a new and deeper way. Now, when I retire at night, I give love, I take love, with my mind, with my heart. Then I fall asleep peacefully.

This big net of giving and receiving got me thinking about the idea of transforming pain into a spiritual practice. My pain, and Victoria's life, I reasoned, may as well be used for good in the world. After a while, and not a long while, it simply was not enough to feel the pain. I wanted to put it to work. As a journalist I had covered the Dalai Lama's visit to New Jersey in the spring of 1998, before Victoria was conceived. I recalled something His Holiness had written about suffering:

> ...within the framework of the Buddhist path, reflecting on suffering has tremendous importance because by realizing the nature of suffering, you will develop greater resolve to put an end to the causes of suffering and the unwholesome deeds that lead to suffering. And it will increase your enthusiasm for engaging in the wholesome actions and deeds that lead to happiness and joy.

The Dalai Lama also wrote in *The Art of Happiness* about the practice of Tong-Len, or giving and receiving, a meditation designed to generate a compassionate state of mind. It goes like this: Mentally visualize that on one side of you is a group of needy people. Perhaps they are refugees or they are sick. Mentally visualize on the other side of you the prototypical self-centered person who is indifferent to others. Between the two, see yourself. Notice toward which side you are inclined. Mentally take on the suffering of the needy group and project your successes, virtues, and love in its direction.

I liked this bridging of the emotional, mental, and physical worlds. When I am lonely for my daughter, I still go to the place where we are both alive—the spirit world—to commune with her. When I return I find my ability to connect to everyone and everything here—the suffering and the joy—is so enhanced that I embrace it all on impulse, not after reflection, as I did before Victoria.

Before Victoria I never let myself feel other people's pain too deeply. Why had I tuned it out? When I was about twelve my parents took my brother and me on a trip to Asia, visiting Thailand, Japan, and Hong Kong. Those were mind-shaping, eye-opening trips.

One day the four of us took two boats out on one of Bangkok's many rivers. The waters were brown, partially from human waste. With one hand I held onto the new camera bag slung over my shoulder. The sun beat down on my lily white arms and legs, exposed by my pink sundress, and sweat trickled between my neat pigtails. As my boat moved forward I gripped both sides. Naked boys and girls dove into the murky water and swam to us. They hung off the sides of our boats, reaching for coins. My father gave me coins and I gave the money to them. The guide talked as we floated down the river until we came to a town whose name I do not remember although I have not forgotten what I saw there. People lived in shacks on stilts on the river's edge. Women washed clothes while children relieved themselves in the same waters.

That night we went back to our hotel, enjoyed a big dinner and watched beautiful Thai women glide through the exotic Dance of the Nails with long gold sheaths on each of their fingers. Glowing stakes of fire surrounded the dance floor. When the performance ended we returned to our hotel suite and continued our comfortable and safe visit amidst pain and poverty.

My life had been like that, a life of privilege. I had met people, written about them, photographed them, given them things. I had offered a compassionate ear or a helping hand, but then I always returned to the Hilton, to safety and comfort. I had seen pain and always sought to understand metaphysically, politically, and socially why it existed. I could say I spent decades wondering why the children in Bangkok were in the water and I in the canoe but never did I *feel* their pain. Never that. I did not know that understanding is found in the feeling and that both come in a rush. I know now.

One Saturday, months after Victoria's death, when I was running errands, I had a conversation about my daughter in every place I went about town. Perhaps I spoke as much as a mother talks about her live child. As I waited at the local pharmacy for the watchmaker, Frank, to pop a new battery into my Seiko, we chatted. In the course of our friendly conversation, I asked him if the two little twin girls pictured on his worktable were his granddaughters. "No, I don't have any granddaughters. They are the granddaughters of Louise, the other watchmaker who shares my workbench," he said. Then he shared his life.

"I got married at seventeen and my wife died at nineteen. I got married again and had two beautiful daughters but my second wife died at forty-two. When my daughters were twenty-two and thirty, the twenty-two-year-old was killed when driving to work one day. She was hit head-on by a drunk driver. When the thirty-year-old heard the news, she had a heart attack and died." Frank peered at me over his magnifiers and glasses. "Watch over your children." I told him it already was too late for that. "One thing I learned," he said. "Don't look over your shoulder. What's the point?" He closed the back of my watch with a click. "Just keep looking ahead."

I wondered, *What would it be like to lose all those people?* Yet Frank appeared calm and happy and liked chatting with his customers. In previous conversations he had revealed a passion for cooking and inviting his neighbors for dinner, and taking vacations on cruise ships. In short, Frank got along "just fine." As I stepped onto the sidewalk, I thought, *All of us have only so much time, including me. Not a minute of it is for wallowing in what could have been.* Victoria, of all people, would not like wallowing. Victoria, who hadn't gotten one second to breathe the air, would appreciate the preciousness of time.

In that moment my heart fluttered and something heavy took flight. The heaviness flew off me and lifted like a bird from a tree, like a feather in a wind. I thought, *Something has ascended to the Father as if on the wings of an angel.*

Another blessing came to me in that first year of healing from my friend Karen whose spiritual practice included participating in a weekly shaman circle. She asked if I would give her circle permission to "journey" with the intention of finding the spirit of Victoria to see how she was, where she was, and with whom. Karen said she wanted to ask Victoria questions about how much pain she was in when she left this world and even if she had wanted to leave. In response to this unusual request, I decided any out-pouring of spiritual attention toward my daughter, be it Buddhist, Catholic, Jewish, Muslim or shamanic, was fine by me. My fate had taught me: The differences do not matter.

Later, Karen reported that she and her shamanic circle took a journey, which they described as a soul trip to places within the self and beyond physical reality. The state of consciousness needed to take such a journey is brought on by drumming and meditating. Using these tools, the journeyers take leave of this world and enter another that my friend describes as rich with imagery and insight. Karen and two others went on a spiritual search for Victoria and later taped their individual experiences for Bill and me to hear since the two of us were not present for the ceremony.

Karen spoke of mentally emerging in the "lower world" where she encountered an image of the Virgin Mary standing among little children playing at her feet. In Mary's hand was a ball of light that shone white and gold. That ball was Victoria. "The spirit of Victoria," Karen said, "gave me a poem for you and Bill."

> *Look for me in the colors of the sunset*
> *for know that you colored my world as I colored*
> *   yours.*
> *Listen for me in the clear true notes of music*
> *   lifting my heart and my spirit.*
> *Feel me in your heart, in the love, in the longing.*
> *Know life touches life as I touched others unmet.*
> *Know this is the true miracle of creation.*

"Life touches life as I touched others unmet" were to me like seeds that blossomed into a gorgeous flower. Victoria's life, so brief and yet so full of promise and affection, indeed has touched others. Since I received this poem I have envisioned my book touching and healing the people who read it. For they are, in my mind, the "others unmet."

The image of the ball of light moved me, too. During yoga a week later I was lying quietly on a mat at the end of class. The teacher led us in a meditation in which we visualized a different colored light entering each of the body's energy centers, or chakras. Right away, I detached from the group meditation and envisioned my body as if white light were emanating from it. To my surprise, I saw in my mind's eye a huge ball of white and gold light descend through the ceiling of the auditorium on that cold December night. It came closer and closer until the edges of that ethereal presence touched mine like a cosmic kiss.

Amid these unexpected joys, though, were moments of pure loss. One night as I prepared dinner I tied an apron around my body with ease. When I was in my eighth month of pregnancy, I could barely fit the apron tie around my midriff. The stark realization flashed through my mind once again, *She is gone.*

Later that night I took a walk around my neighborhood. Winter spread across the evening sky in hues of blue from powdery to electric to almost black. There are times night falls inside me like that, slowly and completely. That particular night, under that sky, I realized those dark moments are part of all of our relationships with people we love, incarnate or not.

That first winter after Victoria died I realized the flow of daily life was covering up my experience. New people I met after the stillbirth did not and would not know about Victoria unless I decided to tell them. The reality sunk in: There were people who did not know and even places I could go where no one knew. My life-transforming experience was hidden. *Perhaps Victoria's death is visible in my countenance,* I thought. *Surely it is readable in my eyes if people look into them deeply and long enough. It must be, of course it is, but how many people look deeply into one another's eyes?*

Many grief books talk about closure. People do, too. Karen had taken part in her shaman circle to help bring closure for herself around Victoria's death. I did not want closure. For me, closure meant something ended, but Victoria and I did not end. *To achieve closure, to even want to, would be to end one of the greatest love relationships of my life*, I thought. *Why would I want to do that?* I want peace, surely, but I want growth, too. I want to talk to Victoria, not just about her. I want to walk with her, to trust she is by my side.

So I started a new personal tradition I had read about in a newsletter on loss. I bought a pure white candle to represent Victoria's innocence. It is mint-scented to remind me of her light sweetness. My plan was to light it every day as a way to have Victoria somehow physically present.

One night, a few weeks before Christmas 1999 when Bill was away on a week-long business trip to Canada, I set the table for a solitary dinner, placing the candle near me on the table. For the first time I lit it. As I enjoyed my potpie and potato, I knew I was onto something great. Even when I am an old woman, even if I find myself alone in the world forty years from now, even if my husband and friends are gone, I can sit down on a cold night with a modest dinner, light a candle, and have this communion.

Even though my Victoria lives mostly in some other world, she still is safe inside me. Maybe this is the way we were destined to be together all along. What my cousin Kathy told me is true. This awful heavy tragedy starts to feel, at times, like a rare joy, a gift. A light in my window on a winter night.

CHAPTER FIFTEEN

❀

The Difficult Land of Love and Grief

One of the effects of stillbirth for me is seeing the fragility of life everywhere and holding it more sacred because of that awareness. This new way of seeing the world continues to unfold and deepen with each year. I continue to be inspired with ways to express my kindness and compassion—to live life more deliberately, in the moment.

Not long after I returned to work following Victoria's stillbirth I learned one of my colleagues would be on medical disability for an extended period. It was then I discovered a new impulse. I went into the kitchen and started perusing my recipe files and cookbooks. I decided to prepare some meals for him and deliver them to his house where he was recuperating from surgery.

As I learned about others who were sick, I started doing this for them as well. It took awhile before I consciously realized that I was recreating the food brigade that had been organized for Bill and me in the weeks following

Victoria's death. It took even longer for me to realize that I was including in every package my favorite food from those days when I was recovering after the stillbirth. I was attempting to give someone else, via my kitchen, the consolation that a dish of ziti brought me. In my own way, I was carrying forth Aunt Esther and Uncle Primo's family tradition. My steamy plates of ziti became a way for me to comfort others, to exclaim, "Bella, bella, we have nice pasta and cheese."

In time, I noticed a newfound deliberateness in myself and an attention to detail that seemed to have eluded me in my busy life before Victoria. On a trip to Monhegan Island off the coast of Maine I walked through an old cemetery. When I found a lichen-covered, 150-year-old gravestone marked with just the word "Infant," I placed a rock on top of it. I wanted to show someone cared. There was no witness to my small act of deliberateness except the sky.

One day while writing a story about Abigail Adams for the newspaper, I found myself including that she had had a daughter who died at one-and-a-half. I wondered, *Would most readers have any idea of how great a loss this must have been for her and her husband, John Adams? In what ways did the death of their child change their lives irrevocably?* Then I sat back in my chair, the computer screen glowing before me, and mused, *How amazing to feel such connections across experiences, across time.*

I continue to live differently since Victoria's death. Recently, I cleaned around a spider nest in my laundry room and realized afterward I had not wanted to disturb

mama spider's brood. Last summer robins made a nest atop
a light at the back of our house. My husband and I were
careful the whole time they stayed to keep the light off
lest we burn the robin family. I wrote a poem about the
nest which, in what I now call my "pre-Victorian days," I
might not have noticed at all:

> A mother robin built a nest
> atop a light under our eaves.
> She sat, watchful,
>   protecting her baby,
>   not knowing she'd chosen
>   a place where the parents' nest
>   had been emptied.
> The safest place.
> The family flew off,
>   left their house of twigs
>   and dirt and straw.
>
> The mother could not have known
> we'd save her nest
>   on the concrete wall
>   of the back stoop
>   where the light shines on it at night
>   and we stop to marvel
>   a bird grew up there
>   and flew away
> And was all right.
>
> It restored our faith,
>   this robin's nest,
>   this triumph of
>   the natural order,
> And we were all right
>   at last.

Another change for me since the stillbirth is the knowledge that refusing to reach out compassionately to one another is the real break in the order of the universe, much more so than a baby's dying. I do not regret that my pain is great because I have had to grow larger to encompass it—it was in this sorrow that love came to me. Without my pain I would not have my precious communions, great and small, for which I would not trade all the heavenly bodies.

For example, my husband and I went to his twentieth college reunion in 2000, a pleasant event complete with cookouts, outdoor bands, and big tents. When Bill played with the fifteen-month-old girl of one of his classmates, my enjoyment came to a halt. *He's supposed to be playing with Victoria*, I thought. I left the tent for the Class of '80 to compose myself and encountered boys playing ball. One saw my tear-stained face. I tried to walk by quickly but he stopped me, held out a white plastic cup and said, "Lady, you can have my soda." My tenderness had engaged his.

The friends who light my inner life now are a marvel. A spring sun shone the day I met a stillbirth mom at a local diner to talk. When we had finished I stepped into the warmth of the day, one arm filled with yellow long-stem roses, a gift from this grateful mom. I placed the flowers on the passenger seat of my car next to a photograph of David, a dear friend and teacher who recently had died and whose picture I had just had framed. David's image smiled back at me with confidence and trust amidst the yellow roses from a new friend.

Something about those fiery roses and portrait made me think of the eternal flame at President John Kennedy's grave at Arlington National Cemetery. David's flame had sparked my heart and mind. All our flames are passed in many ways—from parent to child, from child to parent, from lover to lover, friend to friend, sometimes from stranger to stranger. Often the ignition happens when we do not anticipate it. The wonder in life is never knowing who will accept our individual flame, make it brighter and keep it safe. I have Victoria's flame and now I have David's and that of others, too. I have come to believe that this is the stuff of which peaceful lives and deaths are made.

Superficial relationships no longer take root on my inner landscape. Neither does small talk or feigned affection. If I am to keep my bond with my daughter, I must hold myself in the difficult land where love and grief evoke each other. These two feelings fast entwine because, as Erica Jong writes, "We only grieve where we have loved, and only love where there is the potential for grief." In this land everyone knows loss and emptiness and the only rules of relationship are emotional honesty, respect, and compassion. It is a quiet land because those who meet here listen more than they speak. Those who come are not just other stillbirth parents. Many roads can lead people who understand loss to each other.

In May 2000 I interviewed a Korean War veteran for a feature article on Memorial Day. He lived in a one-room cramped senior citizens' apartment facility. He took his prized possessions out of a box he kept under his bed—a medal and a tattered book his church had given him before he went abroad, *Prayer Book for Soldiers*. Instantly I thought there should be a *Prayer Book for Mothers with Babies in Heaven*. The veteran told me about not sleeping at night during summer storms because thunder sounds like gunfire. I felt a bond with this veteran and the death he had witnessed. The feeling took me by surprise. *Whence did this feeling come?* I asked myself. I had written dozens of stories about veterans in my career but never really felt a bond with any of them.

While driving back to the newspaper I realized this veteran's experiences, like mine, had required blood sacrifice. Maybe to have participated in such a sacrifice is an initiation into another mode of being. This had been the case for the veteran and for me. Most people are in the habit of explaining reality, but I felt that in both our experiences reality had explained us.

In the summer of 2001, after I had penned a version of this book, I accepted an eleventh-hour assignment to interview a Vietnam veteran, Brad Kennedy, who had written a novel, *Heroes or Something*, based on his war experiences. Up against a tight deadline, I had to rely on Brad to tell me about his book. The title referred to how American soldiers who served in Vietnam were treated when they came home, but by the time we finished the extraordinary interview, I was well past the context of the war.

While telling me about comrades who had fallen thirty-five years earlier and recounting battles in which he had played a part, Brad cried. I was stunned at how long he had stayed in his personal jungle of pain and loss, at how loyal he had been to the comrades and truths he had found there. Those truths he would not bury, though he had buried a lot of people, illusions, and expectations about life, and he had the ghosts to show for it. I was mesmerized by the vividness of his memories of so long ago because I knew only love could preserve them so sharply.

Brad fashioned his lead character, Will Stone, after himself, and another character, Captain Mike, after a real-life captain with whom he had served. Brad described this captain as "the Great Captain Mike," the well-loved leader who brought solidarity and strength to the troops. Smiles flickered over Brad's face like weak candlelight when he spoke about a key scene in his book.

After an ambush, the protagonist, Will, went to retrieve dead and wounded American soldiers. There were two dead men in a field, one tall, one short, their bodies propped up next to each other as if they were sitting. Will grabbed the tall corpse from the front and wrapped his arms around the dead man's torso as he attempted to heft the soldier over his shoulder. But Will could not get a grip. The tighter he held the dead man, the more the corpse slid down. Finally, Will realized his hands were not around the fallen soldier, but were inside the soldier's hot, sticky, bloody back. Only when Will was able at last to place this body gently alongside the others ready for evacuation, and then catch a glimpse of that soldier's face and nametag, did he realize it was Captain Mike.

My heart raced and my mind went to that white, numb place that absorbs horror—the place that had felt the shock of holding the corpse of a beloved. Brad reached for his handkerchief and I sat suspended between eras, experiences, emotions, and spiritual dimensions. There was a transcendental moment when I realized Brad's emotional place and my place were similar. It was a place where potentially all people could meet. In every sense of the word, Brad was a hero to me by virtue of how he had honored his whole grisly experience by writing his novel with great honesty.

After that interview, I wondered, *Could our different backgrounds and experiences really have brought us to the same place?* Only when I carefully read that passage in the book some time later did I discover there was more to the Captain Mike story. After Will Stone arose from depositing his captain's body with dignity, he grasped for the strength to go on recovering the dead and wounded from the next burnt-out vehicle and those after that. Where he found that strength is best revealed in the novel's text:

> *Then he thought of Captain Michaels. Just do it, he thought. And he did. He did it, because it needed to be done. He did it, because it was his duty. Most of all, though, he did it because he knew that Captain Mike would have been the first to do likewise, so to do so was to honor his memory, to count him.*
>
> *Will strained to shoulder a body from the next overturned truck.*

Those were the same meanings I found in my experience—none of us lives or dies alone. We carry each other on our shoulders, in our hearts, in our memories, and in this way we are all eternally one.

What relief to have found a well-seasoned traveler in the land of love and grief, a soldier of life who had never forgotten those who fought and fell around him. Brad's hard, true vision of things progressively had deepened his appreciation for how difficult it is to be human and how essential it is to love those we hold near and dear—be they absent or present. Such is Brad's legacy. Such is mine.

I now know I will survive only in the breasts of others. Nature has deprived me of my heir, so the footprints I leave on this world will be spiritual, but no less real. They will lead all who follow to a tender, fertile place beyond compare where family and friends alike abide the first principle of life—to reach out and care for one another. Echoing throughout the land of love and grief is the lesson of stillbirth: Love all those near and dear and never stop.

CHAPTER SIXTEEN

❀

Four Years Later

*T*have not conceived another child, despite trying naturally to do so. My husband and I ruled out using Western fertility medicine. The stillbirth gave us an instinctive understanding that we did not want nature to be forced into doing what it does not want to do. We explored adoption but never started the process. As time goes on and we grow older that option is less likely. The truth is we wanted *that* child. Bill and I came to realize the experience of parenthood we wanted included the biological aspect.

The two of us have changed considerably and perhaps differently. We continue to change. I have processed my experience with my pen, with words that I bring to the world. Bill, however, has had a quieter transformation. He has turned to his creativity, his music, and stays close by my side as a quiet endearing partner who loves and misses Victoria equally.

In October 2003 I was invited to read from my manuscript at a hospital I had never visited. "Walk to Remember" is an annual event at Good Samaritan Hospital in Suffern, New York, to honor babies who died in utero or as newborns. Bill agreed to go. "I want to be there to support you," he said. That day we walked together in the crisp autumn air for a mile up a hill, joining a stream of some three hundred other people who had been pierced with the pain of a stillbirth. All of us carried a balloon, either blue or pink. On our pink balloon we had written in black marker, "Victoria Helen Ash, 6/2/99."

At the top of the hill was a garden with fifteen trees, one to commemorate the children lost in each of the past fifteen years. Winding its way through the trees and grass was a brick walkway. Engraved into many of the bricks were the names of individual babies and the dates of their birth/deaths. I wanted to follow this red brick road, like Dorothy in *The Wizard of Oz*, straight to heaven.

When Bill stepped onto the walkway, he was dabbing his teary eyes. While I read, he listened and followed the program. At the end we released our balloons along with everyone else and the sky filled with pink and blue orbs rising like spirits. The sight of Victoria's balloon moving farther out of our reach made me cry. "Look, Bill," I said, "look how far away she is." Bill wept openly, too, and we held one another as we grieved for our daughter.

That afternoon we expressed publicly for a brief time what we always feel as we walk through our days since the stillbirth—helplessness, smallness in the midst of some great fate, and a longing that will never be sated. We miss Victoria's physical presence, we mourn who she could have been, and we always will.

Let there be no mistake: Finding peace and creating a meaningful life in the aftermath of a stillbirth is no easy task. Our life together is permeated by a profound disappointment that does not go away and does not diminish.

Today the thought of Victoria can still bring Bill to tears. As this manuscript in its progressive stages of editing rolls off our printer, sometimes he reads chapters and breaks down, crying. Victoria has changed him. He will tell anyone who asks—and hardly anyone does—that his fuse is longer, his disposition calmer, since she died. Victoria has given her daddy a new perspective about what is worth getting upset about.

Since Victoria's death Bill has devoted much more time to playing and writing music. I believe he thinks of the time he spends on his art as sacred because it is, in a way, a gift from her. If Victoria were here he would be playing with her, walking with her, telling her who he is, explaining the world. But she is not, so he honors his daughter in the only way he knows—by fully being the loving and artful man she would have known.

In subtle ways both of us keep our hearts—and our proverbial lines—open to Victoria. We could drop the email address Bill made for her in the spring of 1999, before her delivery. He thought it would be cute to send loved ones messages from Victoria along with pictures of her development. We still have that email address, which we never use. Why? Maybe we hope for some Twilight Zone message from her through the mysterious channels of cyberspace. Perhaps it is one small physical reminder that she is in our lives, every day.

We could convert Victoria's nursery into some other type of room but we do not. Why? We do not discuss it. Instead we tacitly let it be. It is an unspoken knowing that we both want to have a space in our home for our daughter. This is Victoria's house, too. Yet, we are also open to the day when this need may change and our expression and acknowledgment of Victoria's life may look different. As Bill and I plan a renovation of our house next year, we do not envision a nursery in it. The so-called new house will be a place where two artists live contentedly, a house with studios and perhaps a meditation room instead of a playroom and a nursery. One day it will not be the home where Victoria would have grown up. But for now, four years after the stillbirth, it is.

Sometimes I sense the world is less interested in us than it would have been if Victoria were here. We have no charming darling who runs into people's arms, whom they can play with and dote over. Some people with children wonder what our lives can possibly be about after Victoria's stillbirth. If they asked—and hardly anyone does—we would tell them it is a full life, but filled in a way to which they are not accustomed.

The truth is many of our relationships did not withstand the test of the stillbirth. Some friends who had been with us right after Victoria died eventually grew impatient with our grief and the evolution of our new selves. They simply could not exist in this new territory. When I look at the situation from their vantage point, I comprehend their confusion. They knew and liked us as we were, but the old Lorraine and Bill are gone now.

I have become a person whose piercing gaze, slower pace, and honesty can make others uncomfortable. While I comprehend why some of my old friends distanced themselves from me, others I do not understand. People I had known for decades suddenly stopped speaking to me altogether after the stillbirth. No sympathy card, no flowers, no phone call. I do not understand people who cut off vital affections at the very point they are most needed. I also do not understand those who gloss over the death of a baby or, for that matter, the death of anyone. By the end of 2003 I had become comfortable in answering what is at first a dreaded question for a stillbirth parent: Do you have any children? I do not miss a beat. "Yes," I say. "I have a daughter who died."

My patience with talking to other stillbirth parents seems endless. Knowing we all need others willing to reach out, listen, and understand, I trained to be a peer counselor to other women who share my fate. In March

2003 I returned home from work to find a message on my answering machine from a stillbirth mom, Julie, whose daughter, Isabella Rose, had died a week earlier. "I feel I don't fit in the world," she confided. In an instant I emotionally flew back to June 1999. I understood that feeling of not fitting in a world of happy people whose children live and for whom nature is a good and righteous thing. In that world stillbirth mothers are aberrations.

Julie had moved to New Jersey from the West Coast with her husband and two-year-old daughter just a few months before her other daughter's stillbirth. She had not yet settled physically into her new home when faced with the emotional and spiritual disruption of stillbirth. Her spirit was dangling, unsettled, between this dimension and the next one where her Isabella had gone. Julie was at the earliest stages of grief when emotions rage like fire, destroying as they go old beliefs and expectations.

"I feel so bad," she said, sobbing. "Maybe my baby is mad at me because I let her die." Julie shared her concern that she had somehow "upset" her Isabella into dying while in utero because Julie had had an argument with somebody. I understood. After Victoria's stillbirth, I scrutinized every aspect of my life looking for that one incident, that one moment when I may have caused the stillbirth. I even wondered if I had killed Victoria because I had eaten imported provolone cheese! I had admonished myself for having eaten anything "foreign."

Another mother I met wondered if by assuming some simple yoga pose she had somehow doomed her baby. Though irrational, such thoughts surface naturally when grappling with a stillbirth and its causes, even though I certainly knew that my body had betrayed me.

I listened to Julie for a long time, her conversation filled with tears, sobs, and regrets, as she expressed her most profound grief. I shared with her some wisdom I had garnered by walking for the past four years through my own pain, transformation, and healing.

> *You will keep seeing the world differently from this time forward. You will speak, feel, and love differently. Isabella is the difference between your old self and your new one. Isabella will be the intangible presence in every beauty you behold. She will be the light over the mesa, the sound of the water in the bay at night, the memory of a years-old embrace that still brings you comfort. Now I think of the wind as the breath of every baby who was never born.*

The very day I got Julie's call a friend at the newspaper had announced the arrival of her niece, who had been born in Korea nine months earlier and recently adopted by my friend's brother and sister-in-law. "Her name is Isabella," my friend beamed, "and her new family—mother, father, and brother—thank God for her." I stood in my living room and played Julie's message again. In that moment the reality of my life struck me. *Here is my place in the world—the void between the mothers of these two baby girls. I feel one's pain as acutely as the other's joy. I embrace them both with the knowledge they represent the span of human experience and the faith that different blessings can flow from each.*

After the Isabella connections, I began to wonder if this painful fate of mine, so useful in helping others, is about something even more. I concluded, *The only way to live my life is to love this fate because it is mine, because it was entrusted to me.* For me, such love must burn for itself whether there is a divine plan or not, whether there is divinity or not. Without this great pain I would not have found myself capable of truly loving what is lost and, by extension, what is still here. Without this great pain I would have kept trying to conquer my vulnerabilities instead of sharing them with others. Without this great pain I would not understand that love does not require breath.

In speaking with Julie I even came to understand that I was as much helped by giving to her as she was sharing with me. Never again can I believe there are those of us who help and those of us who are helped. We are all both. Never again can I believe in the divisions that supposedly separate any of us.

There is an ancient metaphor the Indian rishis use to explain who people really are. It has brought me great comfort in reflecting on my own pain and loss, and the larger sense of my life.

Picture buckets in the sun, each filled with water, each standing for one human being—the buckets represent our bodies, and the water represents our minds. Each bucket reflects the sun beating down from above, the sun being the divine consciousness that pervades us all. The sun is not our thoughts but rather the consciousness behind our thoughts. The sun is the overriding spirit through which we notice our thoughts and feelings change.

When a bucket breaks and spills its contents and is done, the sun remains untouched. The sun goes nowhere, just as we do not when we die. It just is, as we are.

When I listened to a Swami explain this metaphor, he said the condition of the water—the condition of our minds—determines how well the sun reflects in us. Reflecting on all of this four years down the road, I now believe that except for the last hours of her life Victoria was content, her water calm, her reflection perfect. I have come to believe, *There was a time when she and I were together under the sun. Now we are the sun.* In this way I believe Victoria and I are still with each other—and with each other is the only way we can be.

I do not believe God loves one family and forsakes another. I do not feel forsaken. The divine presence in the family of a live baby and that of a baby who has died manifests itself in different ways in our hearts.

There is a part of me that knows my daughter remains in just this way. She was conceived in me and she died in me. I carried her temporal body and her spark of eternity. The body is gone, the spark is not. When the water of my mind is clear and calm, the sun warms it and I understand the water, the bucket, the sun, Victoria, myself, and all of us.

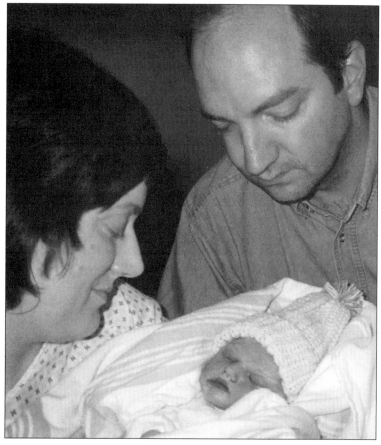

Victoria Helen Ash with her parents, Lorraine and Bill Ash.

ABOUT STILLBIRTH

The National Center for Health Statistics shows that in 2003, the latest year for which figures are available, 25,653 babies died after twenty weeks or more in utero and are considered stillborn. The number declined from 1990, when 31,386 babies were stillborn, perhaps because we stillbirth parents have become vocal about our losses and our grief, raising consciousness for pregnant women brave enough to listen and demand extra care when they sense something is amiss with the child they are carrying. But there is still much work to be done. In 2006, the National Institute of Child Health and Human Development (NICHD) reported stillbirths occur in nearly one in 200 pregnancies in the United States every year.

There are myriad reasons babies are stillborn, among them birth defects, genetic anomalies, maternal infections, umbilical cord accidents, and placenta problems. According to the NICHD, doctors know enough to identify what kills half of the stillborn babies, but they do not know enough to consistently prevent stillbirth. "In spite of how often stillbirth occurs, and how emotionally painful it can be," NICHD officials write, "Little research has been done on this type of pregnancy loss."

Which parents are likely to lose their baby in utero after twenty weeks, sometimes at full term? It is impossible to tell and that is part of the devastation of stillbirth, sometimes called the last mystery of obstetrics. Rich Olsen, a stillbirth father from Arizona who founded The National Stillbirth Society, expresses it well: "Stillbirth is an equal opportunity destroyer of dreams. It cuts across age lines, color lines, race lines, class lines, and all lines. Norman Rockwell-type mothers can have stillbirths and crack mothers can have live births. At present there is no way to predict who will be next. Though stillbirth is as random as lightning strikes in a thunderstorm it is rarely caused by anything the mother did or didn't do during her pregnancy."

In addition to medical reasons for stillbirth, there are other issues that beg to be researched—issues stillbirth parents wonder about as we notice patterns in our experiences:

- Is there a relationship between stress and stillbirth?
- Should there be better monitoring of all mothers after the twentieth week of pregnancy?
- Are some mothers more likely to successfully deliver babies of one gender and not the other?
- Are stillbirth parents more or less likely to adopt, and why?

It is essential that there be ongoing education of medical staff, parents, and the general public about stillbirth. Funding research to find out why some babies are stillborn and how to prevent their deaths must go hand in hand with stillbirth education. The good news is that many stillbirth parents no longer passively allow the medical profession and others to prevent them from seeing or holding their stillborn babies. No longer will stillbirth parents be kept from grieving a real loss, or from questioning what happened to cause the death. Stillbirth parents have formed national networks of support and advocacy; created online memorials to their children; and in some cases provide free medical monitoring equipment to pregnant mothers at home. A healthy discussion of stillbirth is slowly emerging, pulling back the societal veils that have kept it hidden and taboo.

In the past three decades there have been significant steps toward a growing consciousness about stillbirth deaths and advocacy for parents and families faced with this loss and grief.

- In 1977, the international organization, SHARE Pregnancy and Infant Loss Support, began at St. John's Hospital in Springfield, Illinois when a bereaved parent and several hospital staffers insisted on creating a support group. Today SHARE is headquartered in Missouri and has some 130 chapters worldwide.

  Additionally, other organizations have formed to offer stillbirth parents support through a network of regional and local groups. They include Mommies Enduring Neonatal Death, based in Texas, and the M.I.S.S. Foundation (formerly Mothers in Sympathy and Support) in Arizona.

- In 1983, Richard M. Pauli, a medical geneticist at the University of Wisconsin-Madison and father of a stillborn baby, founded the Wisconsin Stillbirth Service Program (WiSSP), which has developed hospital protocols for assessing stillbirths in an attempt to better determine their cause. The protocols are in use throughout Wisconsin and have helped evaluate some 1,600 stillbirths in hopes of identifying new information for future prevention.

- In 1988, President Ronald Reagan proclaimed October as "Pregnancy and Infant Loss Awareness Month." Since then a growing number of hospitals are hosting Walks to Remember. Every October these events honor and openly acknowledge babies lost before birth and during the early months of life.

- In 1990, parents of babies with Group B Streptococcus (GBS), the bacterial infection that killed my daughter, Victoria, formed the Group B Strep Association. Their goal is to raise awareness of the devastation the infection can cause. Some years later, The Jesse Cause took on the same mission. In 2006, Group B Strep International added its voice. This bacteria remains the most common cause of life-threatening infections in newborns, according to the Centers for Disease Control and Prevention. One fourth of pregnant women naturally carry Group B Strep in the vagina or rectum. Most mothers, including me, show no symptoms.

- In 1990, the American College of Obstetricians and Gynecologists and the federal Maternal and Child Health Bureau united to form the National Fetal Infant Mortality Review Program, which reaches out to stillbirth mothers as they leave hospitals to find out what went wrong and to offer grief materials.

- In 2002, the National Sudden Infant Death Syndrome (SIDS) Alliance changed its name to First Candle, reflecting the expansion of its mission to include not only those babies who die of SIDS but also those who are stillborn. The National Stillbirth Society launched the same year.

- In 2003, the NICHD awarded nearly $3 million to fund the Stillbirth Research Collaborative Network, comprising five research centers nationwide and an independent data center to collect and analyze statistics on stillbirth. Other goals of the five-year project include designing studies to explore the causes of stillbirth and developing standardized research guidelines for reporting and studying stillbirths.

- In December 2003, the International Stillbirth Alliance, whose primary goals include becoming a clearinghouse for all stillbirth research worldwide, established a web site. Stillbirth parents founded this group to help promote awareness about stillbirth, and they hold an annual conference to further worldwide awareness of stillbirth issues.
- In Summer 2007, Arkansas became the latest of thirty-one states to offer stillbirth parents either a certificate of stillbirth or a document that includes the words "certificate of birth." The M.I.S.S. Foundation spearheads an effort to convince legislatures, state by state, to pass the "Missing Angels Bills" that make these certificates available. Having such a certificate makes a significant psychological difference for some stillbirth parents. While a certificate of fetal death acknowledges a baby's death, a stillbirth certificate acknowledges a baby's life. In addition, this certificate validates that stillbirth parents are indeed mothers and fathers. "All mothers give birth," notes Olsen of The National Stillbirth Society. "Only the outcomes of those births differ."

Some groups and campaigns have devoted themselves to raising awareness about various individual causes of stillbirth. Among them are The Skye Foundation, which focuses on bleeding disorders related to pregnancy, and the March of Dimes Foundation. All of the steps mentioned have been significant advances in moving the issues of stillbirth to the forefront for further research and open discussion. Today's stillbirth parents have come a long way in sharing our stories and insisting that the medical profession, as well as family and friends, recognize the devastation caused by the stillbirth death of our babies.

Not until the 1970s did parents of stillborn babies even get to see or hold their little darlings after the birth. Now, many do. Still, there is back peddling in the medical community even on that fundamental issue. In 2002, Patricia Hughes, Ph.D., a clinical psychologist at St. George's Hospital Medical School in London, announced the findings of a study involving sixty-five stillbirth mothers. Dr. Hughes claims the small study shows that those who had held their stillborn child had more trouble bonding with their next born child.

This study continues to be criticized publicly by the American stillbirth community because many stillbirth parents know this has not been their experience. These findings fly in the face of the collective wisdom of thousands of stillbirth parents. We know differently. In addition, the findings have been questioned because of inadequate study controls, and the fact that the sample size is too small to make such a sweeping statement about what is best for stillbirth parents.

Fortunately, excerpts from *Life Touches Life* are included in the eighth edition of *Olds' Maternal-Newborn Nursing & Women's Health Across the Lifespan* (Pearson Prentice Hall 2008). I especially like that the authors included the photo of Bill and me holding Victoria, with a photo caption that reads: "Parents holding their deceased infant." In this teaching volume for nurses, there is a wise "Clinical Tip" that reads: "Allow the family to dictate their own experience. A compassionate, caring presence and gentle guidance are often all that is needed to facilitate the family's mourning process." This is hopeful!

Whenever one of my articles about stillbirth is published or I give a lecture or writing workshop on stillbirth, I get calls and mail from stillbirth parents in North America and worldwide, including Turkey, China, Italy, Norway, and Australia. Some are fresh with the pain, such as the young mother from a little town in Illinois who thanked me for listening to her story. But for many who contact me the pain is not fresh. It is very old and veiled with layers of regret and self-reproach. One woman, whose baby had been stillborn in 1965, asked me in a hushed tone, "You mean, this happens for physical reasons?" She had spent the past thirty-seven years thinking she had somehow willed her baby's death.

Another woman who was in her late 70s had returned home from the hospital without her child some forty years earlier. She locked herself in her bedroom and cried for one month. After she emerged, she never breathed a word of the experience to anyone. She did not hold her baby, explore what happened or why, or get the opportunity to have a grave or funeral. Basically, there was no way she could process her feelings. She had lived with the grief frozen around her heart for four decades.

It is for the sake of women like these, as well as for the almost 26,000 stunned and hurt mothers who join their ranks every year in the United States, that this book is written. It is for the mothers of stillborn babies all around the world. It is also for all the fathers of stillborn babies; for all the grandparents; for everyone who loved the unborn, sight unseen; and for every baby who never got to draw a breath.

I pray all of us will someday be reunited with the children who have somehow been lost to us in the stars. But I know that, by turning to each other now to do all we can to understand and stop stillbirth, our angels' lives, however brief, will not have been in vain.

—LORRAINE ASH
September 2007

Resources

Stillbirth parents can become involved in these groups and initiatives, each listed with its state of origin. Many have chapters and memberships that span multiple states and have more than one mission. All listings updated as of September 2007.

- ## Advocacy
  First Candle, Maryland, www.firstcandle.org

  The National Stillbirth Society, Arizona, www.stillnomore.org

- ## Education/Awareness
  Gateway Northwest Maternal and Child Health Network, New Jersey, www.gatewaymch.org

  Group B Strep Association, North Carolina, www.groupbstrep.org

  Group B Strep International, California, www.groupbstrepinternational.org

  The Jesse Cause, California, www.thejessecause.org

  RTS Bereavement Training, Wisconsin, www.bereavementprograms.com

  SHARE Pregnancy and Infant Loss Support, Missouri, www.nationalshareoffice.com

  The Skye Foundation, New Jersey, www.theskyefoundation.org

USAID, The U.S. Agency for International Development, Maternal and Child Health, Washington, D.C., http://www.usaid.gov/our_work/global_health/mch/mh/faqs.html

- EMOTIONAL SUPPORT
Aiding Mothers and Fathers Experiencing Neonatal Death (AMEND), Missouri, www.amendgroup.com

Center for Loss in Multiple Birth (CLIMB), Alaska, www.climb-support.org

The Compassionate Friends, Illinois, www.compassionatefriends.org

Different Kind of Parenting, Washington, www.kotapress.com/section_home/parentingZine_intro.htm

Faith's Lodge, Wisconsin, www.faithslodge.org

Joining In Memory, Kentucky, www.ucumberlands.edu/lamentations

M.I.S.S. Foundation, Arizona, www.missfoundation.org

Missing GRACE Foundation, Minnesota, www.missinggrace.org

Mommies Enduring Neonatal Death, Texas, www.mend.org

Mothers of Angels, Arkansas, www.mothersofangels.org

Pregnancy Loss & Infant Death Alliance, Colorado, www.plida.org

- FINANCIAL ASSISTANCE
Angel Names Association, New York, www.angelnames.org

The Tears Foundation, Washington, www.thetearsfoundation.org

- HELP FOR RELATIVES AND FRIENDS
  Remembering Our Babies, Texas, www.october15th.com

- POLITICAL ACTION
  Missing Angels Bills, Arizona, www.missingangelsbill.org

- RESEARCH
  International Stillbirth Alliance, Maryland, www.stillbirthalliance.org

  National Fetal Infant Mortality Review Program, Washington, D.C., www.acog.org/from_home/departments/dept_web.cfm?recno=10

  Stillbirth Collaborative Research Network of the National Institute of Child Health and Human Development, Maryland, www.nichd.nih.gov/research/supported/scrn.cfm

  Wisconsin Stillbirth Service Program, Wisconsin, www.wisc.edu/wissp

ACKNOWLEDGMENTS

I owe so much to so many. My deep thanks to Maureen Michelson, NewSage Press publisher, for her courage, vision and willingness to publish a story of stillbirth, showing the world a corner of the human experience that too many have neglected for too long. The manuscript benefited from her sharp editing talent and understanding heart. Thanks to NewSage book designer Sherry Wachter, who gave *Life Touches Life* its beautiful face.

I am profoundly grateful as well to Dr. Christiane Northrup, who wrote the foreword and whose guardian grace over this story and personal support revived my spirit on more than one occasion. To be on the receiving end of her refreshing blend of compassion, open-mindedness, and enthusiasm is a delight and a privilege. Thanks also to John O'Donohue and his assistant, Barbara Connor, as well as Dr. Larry Dossey and authors John Welshons and Adam Pertman for bolstering this work with endorsements.

For encouraging me in my most vulnerable and unsteady days, I thank Mark Delude, a compassionate man and my true and constant companion who listened to me unfailingly and patiently during the first two years after the stillbirth. He coaxed me to let my pen express the pain in my heart.

For the title, I thank Karen Phelps for delivering from places unknown to me the pure literary treasure that is the poem, *Life Touches Life*, from which this work gets its title. I thank Lone Jensen for guidance and support.

I am indebted, too, to other wonderful writers who gave so much of their time, effort and love to this project. Pat Carr, my literary mother, taught me how to tell a tale such as this, for which I will forever be grateful, and lent a steady and wise hand in the beginning drafts.

I thank Brad Kennedy for his friendship and for his support of *Life Touches Life* from the moment he read it. I thank him for long sessions in his office, into the wee hours, poring over individual sentences and passages to ensure they were as precise as they could be in the expression of complex emotions and thoughts. Never have I known such congruence of spirit and mind on the page.

I thank, too, those who have told me wise things about writing over the years, including my eighth-grade English teacher, Sister Mary Michele of Saint Philip the Apostle School in Saddle Brook, New Jersey, and, in my adult years, R. David Cox and George Gordon, neither of whom lived to hold this book in his hands. I hold them both in my heart.

Many thanks to Krys Toczylowski and Alissa Sandler, bereavement counselors at Hackensack University Medical Center who helped me and my family through the first days of shell shock, and to all the nurses on the maternity ward there who compassionately cared for me in my weakest hours and who tenderly dressed, powdered and cradled the body of my daughter, Victoria. Thanks to Dr. Gerard Hansen for saving my life, for displaying aplomb under pressure, for personally serving me orange juice in my hospital bed and for saying all the right things at the right time, starting from the hour we learned my daughter had died in utero.

I thank my parents, Victor and Julia Mullica, for imparting to me solid moral and emotional sustenance all my life and for being as sensitive and supportive as parents can be during this sad crisis even as they, too, suffered. I thank my cousin, Kathy Stanwood, for holding my hand and lighting the path in the very darkest days.

I thank Christine Nunn and my mother-in-law, Joan Ash, for calling me every Mother's Day. I thank Carol Nunn and Sally Montgomery for remembering Victoria every Christmas. Such endurance is not to be taken for granted.

With all my heart, I thank my husband, Bill, for without his constant presence, watchfulness, and love, sheer fright may have overcome me.

Finally, I thank my muse, Victoria Helen, whose brief and beautiful life has redirected mine in all good ways. Piccolina, Mommy will always love you.

—LORRAINE ASH
January 2004

About the Author

Helen Ash / Glen Roc Photography

Lorraine Ash has been working as a newspaper journalist since 1982, currently for the *Daily Record* in Parsippany, New Jersey. Her feature articles and series, particularly on health and women's issues, have won national, state, and regional awards and appeared in daily newspapers across the country.

Her three plays, each about a U.S. president, *Monroe, Jackson* and *Tyler,* are published by *The History Project,* based in Galax, Virginia. An essayist whose works have appeared in various literary journals, Ash currently is co-writing a book exploring how life's big questions filter down into the everyday decisions people make.

Since earning a master's degree in Communications from Fordham University, she has studied writing at various venues, including the Wesleyan Writers Conference in Connecticut, the Fine Arts Work Center in Massachusetts, and the American Society of Journalists and Authors in New York. She has taught writing on the college level and is a member of The International Women's Writing Guild.

Ash lives in Allendale, New Jersey, with her husband, Bill, a jazz trumpeter. Her passions include Hindu philosophy, bookstores and libraries, good food, fitness, and the state of Maine. As a peer grief contact, she works one-on-one with stillbirth mothers. This is her first book.

Contact Lorraine Ash at www.lorraineash.com, email:
lifetoucheslife@lorraineash.com
or write to her at P.O. Box 200, Allendale, NJ 07401-0200

OTHER BOOKS BY NEWSAGE PRESS

*N*ewSage Press publishes nonfiction books on a variety of topics. The following books address death and grief. For a complete list of our titles, including chapter excerpts, visit our website: www.newsagepress.com

---

BOOKS ON HUMAN LOSS

Children Helping Children with Grief: My Path to Founding The Dougy Center for Grieving Children and Their Families
Beverly J. Chappell

Compassion in Dying: Stories of Dignity and Choice
Barbara Coombs Lee, Ed., Foreword by Barbara K. Roberts

Death Without Denial, Grief Without Apology:
A Guide for Facing Death and Loss
Barbara K. Roberts

Common Heroes: Facing a Life Threatening Illness
Eric Blau, M.D.

BOOKS ON PET LOSS

Blessing the Bridge: What Animals Teach Us About Death, Dying, and Beyond
Rita Reynolds, Foreword by Gary Kowalski

Three Cats, Two Dogs, One Journey Through Multiple Pet Loss
David Congalton

NewSage Press
PO Box 607, Troutdale, OR 97060-0607

Phone Toll Free 877-695-2211, Fax 503-695-5406
Email: info@newsagepress.com

Distributed to bookstores by Publishers Group West
800-788-3123